FAMILY CRISIS AS PROCESS

Persistence and Change

Jason Montgomery

UNIVERSITY
PRESS OF
AMERICA

LANHAM • NEW YORK • LONDON

Copyright © 1982 by

University Press of America,™ Inc.

4720 Boston Way
Lanham, MD 20706

3 Henrietta Street
London WC2E 8LU England

Library of Congress Cataloging in Publication Data

Montgomery, Jason.
   Family crisis as process.

   Bibliography: p.
   Includes index.
   1. Family life education. I. Title.
HQ10.M64   306.8   81–40566
ISBN 0–8191–1788–9   AACR2
ISBN 0–8191–1789–7 (pbk.)

To those who have shared with me

the joy of family living

and the anguish of dissolution.

TABLE OF CONTENTS

FOREWORD

This book contains a view of families who are busily getting into trouble and either passively wallowing or actively trying to get out. Although virtually all families run into difficulty, not all, by any means, come out of the experience alive and well and whole. We will take a look at the quick and the dead and those families somewhere in between.

In my travels, I came upon a queer sort of country and observed that it was inhabited by a people with a strange sort of walk. Their pace was such that while on the level they could walk ably enough but when faced with the slightest slope they would trip over their feet and fall face down. Since this land was not exceedingly flat, they were forever falling.

As I watched, one inhabitant came my way and stumbled and fell in front of me. He lay there benumbed for a moment and I asked him what he was thinking. He said, "I am pretending that it hasn't really happened." To my response that his position at my feet indicated otherwise, he replied, "I am sick-unto-death of stumbling but I do not know what to do about it. I suppose I'll have to try again and this time I'll just have to be more careful." He laboriously got to his feet and walked away in that same peculiar manner. I heard his "Left, wiggle, right, slump, left, wiggle, right DAMMIT ALL."

I asked the next prostrate figure what she was going to do about her problem. She said, "I can't stand this any longer. I'm going to leave, to go where the land is flat and I can avoid the ups and downs." The last I saw of her was when she disappeared into the distance. She was clutching her altimeter and cursing the flatness-created boredom of her path.

In further travels I met with many other stumblers and cursers.

But one day, I saw a beautiful sight. In a small and isolated corner of the land was a happy people who could move at will. In their buildings and where it was level, they walked with the usual left-wiggle-right-slump but outside on the hills they turned side ways and walked by stepping with the right foot and drawing up their left, and so on.

I caught up with one of the side walkers and

asked him about it all and we spoke together. He said, "We, too, had developed this stupid way of walking, I can't remember just why, but it served a purpose at one time. As the others in this land, we had fallen continually; we, too, had attempted to exchange boredom for bruise. This solution was not satisfactory, no more satisfactory than covering the land with foam rubber or building a better hospital, solutions that we also tried.

"One day a funny little man came to our village and he said he could help us. He said, 'The fact is that you have a bad situation that you cannot change. None of your solutions make life bearable because their success requires your falling and this is what you wish to change. You need a solution that will enable you to walk upright. So, consider why you fall. You fall because when you walk you cannot pass one foot by the other. To correct the situation you need only to change your gait. Walk sideways not frontwards. Instead of left, wiggle, right, slump, you should walk this way: right, draw up the left foot, right, draw up the left foot, and so forth.'"

"And so we changed but it was not easy. Many thought that side walking was unnatural and wouldn't do it. Others, such as knee patch makers and broken nose specialists, were opposed to change for obvious reasons. Political leaders were mixed in their reaction for they wanted to lead the people but didn't know whether to stand in front or off to the side. Eventually, we successfully convinced almost everyone that the small change in walking was much better than the pain of falling and we changed our lives and enjoy the world more than we ever did before."

Falling down and getting up is what this book is all about for real families have as many difficulties as imaginary foot shufflers in magic lands. Some have long term problems which emanate from the personality mix that has characterized the family from its beginning. Others have problems dropped on them as a result of unusual man-made or natural disasters. Virtually all families must manage problems brought about by the growth of persons and the attendant changes in family relationships.

Whatever the source, families must deal with the problem and they usually do so alone. Some, like the first person in the narrative, will blindly try again without making any change. Others will leave the problem-related field and search for a better life elsewhere. These may be successful or not. Others, like those in the favored village, will find a way to resolve their difficulty and

viii

make the changes that will allow them to stay together and be satisfied. The aim of this book is to specify the family's resources which help it to endure, to satisfy the needs of its members, and to meet its social obligations.

I am saying that from time to time, families must change their relationship patterns and, when this is required of them, stress usually results. Stress facilitates the study of family interaction because automatic processes become conscious and a family's hidden ways are exposed. Stress also places families at risk. Therefore, the study of families-in-crisis is important because the stress-exposed patterns are more likely to be apparent and because it is the time when families need self understanding or professional help.

The object of the book is to explore the internal workings of families that are in crisis situations. The book attempts to isolate, name, and classify the family's characteristics that are particularly important to the generation and resolution of crisis. As the title indicates, the book explores a family's need to change, why it has difficulty in doing so, and the price it pays for this reluctance. The object of inquiry is not individuals, or society, it is the family itself, especially the relationships which affect its relative success in dealing with the stressful times associated with changes in personnel, relationships, and context.

The book is not a simple one. The dynamic qualities of family life are complex, ever changing, and well hidden behind social and family myths. It takes time and effort to accurately perceive and correctly understand the nature of family life. It is, I believe, well worth the effort for our personal satisfaction and our social well-being grow from family intimacies.

Have a good trip.

A few words about the book and its organization. Essentially, the book presents a model of family interaction; that is, the book is my description in diagrams and words of how families get in and out of critical situations. Chapter 1 gives the theoretical basis for the crisis model and in Chapters 2,3,4, and 5, the model is presented. Each chapter will end with a summary statement regarding the family's strengths (as indicated by the model) which help them to successfully meet the challenges associated with crisis. The last chapter will indicate the uses of the model and suggest some directions for subsequent theoretical development and practical application.

The book was written for use by students of family life. It assumes that a reader will have a background which includes psychology, sociology, and some knowledge of the special area of family dynamics. Chapter 1 includes material which will either introduce basic information or refresh memories related to fundamental material; its goal is to have students begin inquiry with at least a common perspective if not a common understanding of background material. If a student finds that they are having difficulty with the material in Chapter 1, he or she would be well advised to further study the source material as that is indicated in the footnotes.

To get the most out of this book, students should keep in mind four ideas. The first of these is that the model is an attempt to explain what is behind that which we can observe. I mean, it is clear and can be observed that families are more or less successful in remaining intact and functional and the model explains why this is so. That is, it describes the characteristics that are associated with success and non-success.

This brings us to the second point: the book is complicated. The book's complexity arises from our basic ignorance of the processes associated with crisis. That is, we do not know which of the family's characteristics is the most important in getting a family involved in crisis and which contributes most to getting it out. So, this model must indicate as many of the salient attributes as possible; later, their relative importance can be determined.

The complexity of my approach may appear to muddy the waters of understanding but there is no other way. Until now, we have had partial views of the process and so our understanding has only been partial, however clear it may have been. I have seen my contribution as being the synthesis of these partial views and the addition of my own insights. The product is, hopefully, a complete picture of the crisis process, one which considers families prior to the stressor, stays with them during their reaction to the stressor, and explores issues associated with their patterns of reorganization. Admittedly, the result is sometimes complicated, perhaps overly so and yet, the next step of simplification requires this complexity for without it there is nothing to simplify and no parameters within which the simplification can take place.

A third point is that the book's object of inquiry is the family. Although families are composed of people and fit into a social setting, my focus is on the family. For example: the book emphasizes the family's decision making process rather than the thoughts of the people involved or the impact on society. I am not concerned with the conscious or unconscious thought processes of family members for these thought processes are not at the family level; I am concerned with the process of decision making and its effect on the family's ability to deal successfully with its problem. In reading the book, I suggest you focus on the family as well.

The last point I wish to make is that you would do well to consider this book as only a description of involved processes and my description at that. Being the product of my mind, it is necessarily both limited and tentative. It is theory which has been regarded in the light of my experience of my life (yes, in some ways it is a personal document) and the lives of others with whom I have come in contact. It is tentative in that it is my first word rather than my last. I expect the model to develop and to become more powerful as an explanatory device and more concise in its presentation.

Earlier versions of this manuscript were read and critiqued by Michael Lewis of the University of Massachusetts and Dianne Kieren of the University of Alberta. Several hundred students who have taken my family crisis course have also contributed ideas. I am indebted to these fellow inquirers for their interest, their comments, and their support.

Barbara Sykes deserves special mention for her assistance in making editorial changes and otherwide guiding to conclusion an earlier version of this manuscript. This assistance and her general support I appreciate beyond words.

CHAPTER 1

STARTING POINTS

To understand the family in crisis it is necessary to understand persistence and change.[1] Crisis consists of the events associated with the family's necessity to change and its difficulty in doing so. Over time, families develop patterns of action and interaction and these patterns require revision as either the family or its environment changes. Revision is difficult for the patterns that must be changed are entrenched and supported by other parts of the family system. The family's problem is that they must revise its way of doing things yet this revision is difficult.

This generates three questions:
Why is change in the family necessary?
Why do families change only with difficulty?
What family processes are associated with change?
The book is an attempt to answer these three questions and does so by synthesizing two perspectives; the developmental

---

[1] There are other ways to understand crisis and other models as well. This model draws unblushingly on the stimulating work of others. Some other models of family crisis are: Reuben Hill, "Generic Features of Families under Stress," Social Casework, 39, 1958, pp. 139-150; Bernard Farber, Family: Organization and Interaction (San Francisco: Chandler, 1964), pp. 338-441; Florence Rosenstock and Bernard Kutner, "Alienation and Family Crisis," Sociological Quarterly, 9, 1967, pp. 397-405. Donald Hansen and Reuben Hill, "Families Under Stress," Handbook of Marriage and the Family, (ed.) Harold Christensen (Chicago: Rand McNally & Co., 1964), pp. 782-819. I acknowledge my debt to these and others whose work has provided the basis for this inquiry.

framework[2] and general systems theory.[3] The systems perspective helps us to see why change is difficult; the developmental framework provides insights which help explain the necessity to change. These two perspectives form the book's foundation and I have added to them to broaden its scope- to show the steps that families take as they move through crisis toward reorganizing themselves as adequately functioning intact groups, as static and functionally inadequate families, or as disintegrating units.

In this first chapter, we will consider the developmental approach and the systems perspective as these help us deal with problems of persistence and change. Time, space, and relevance considerations are such that only a brief consideration of the two antecedent perspectives is possible. However, this consideration is necessary because it will lead us to nine ideas which form the basis of this inquiry. The final section of the chapter will provide a definition of family crisis.

---

[2] The developmental framework is expressed in: Joan Aldous, "The Family Developmental Approach to Family Analysis," (Minneapolis, Minnesota: Department of Sociology, 1967); Evelyn Duvall, Family Development (Philadelphia: Lippincott, 1957); Reuben Hill and Donald Hansen, "The Identification of Conceptual Frameworks Utilized in Family Study," Marriage and Family Living, 22, 1960, pp. 299-311; Reuben Hill and Roy H. Rodgers, "The Developmental Approach," Handbook of Marriage and the Family, Christensen, op. cit., pp. 171-211; Francis Magrabi and W.J. Marshall, "Family Developmental Tasks: A Research Model," Journal of Marriage and the Family, 1965, pp. 454-461; Roy Rodgers, "Toward a Theory of Family Development," Journal of Marriage and the Family, 26, 1965, pp. 454-461; Ivan Nye and Felix Berardo, Conceptual Frameworks for the Study of the Family (New York: The Macmillan Company, 1966); Roy Rodgers, Family Interaction and Transaction: The Developmental Approach (Englewood Cliffs, N.J.: Prentice Hall, 1973).

[3] Articles on systems and family systems are: Reuben Hill, "Modern Systems Theory and the Family: A Confrontation," Family Sociology, 1971, pp. 264-283; K. Dean Black, "Systems Theory and the Development of the Marital Relationship," Paper presented at the Annual Meeting of the American Sociological Association, New Orleans, LA., 1972; Walter Buckley, Sociology and Modern Systems Theory (Englewood Cliffs, N.J.: Prentice-Hall, 1967); Salvador Minuchin, Families and Family Therapy (Cambridge, MA.: Harvard University Press, 1976); William Lederer and Don D. Jackson, Mirages of Marriage (New York: Norton, 1969); D.C. Speer, "Family Systems: Morphostasis and Morphogenesis, or Is Homeostasis Enough?" Family Process, 9, 1970, pp. 259-278.

THE DEVELOPMENTAL FRAMEWORK

An important part of the developmental framework is that it is dynamic; it concerns the family's movement through time. In this framework, the family is seen as a unit which changes dramatically with its passage through the years. The family is given an organismic quality with a birth, a childhood, an adolescence, a maturity, and a death. These stages are reflected in the term "family life cycle".

Time within the developmental framework has a different nature than time in the systems approach. In the latter, the emphasis is on the time required to establish a system or the time that a system requires to re-establish a former level of functioning. In the developmental framework, time is regarded in larger units, those associated with the family's life cycle, and time is seen in terms of the changes it brings about.

The developmental framework concentrates attention on change in the family's internal processes, this change being associated with the family's movement through the life cycle. Some processes are related to the family's formation; other processes surround the birth of the first child. When additional children are born into the household, different dynamics are involved. Still other processes are related to the children's leaving home and others are relevant as the family shrinks to two and then to one.

The changes in processes involve both interaction and task performance. First, interaction. Interaction in a family of two is different from interaction in a family of three; the number of relationships jumps from two to six. The kind of interaction varies also. Parenting provides us with an example. The father-son relationship of a twenty-five year old father and his five-year old son is substantially different from that which will exist fifteen years later. As the son ages he will want more independence. So, both the quantity and the nature of interaction vary as the family moves through time.

With the passage of time a family's tasks change also. Tasks in joining (for example, deciding who is to buy what commodities) are different from the tasks of separating (how to divide that which was formerly purchased). Tasks of marriage's early years (such as getting established) are different from the tasks of later years (such as re-forming social life). Although a family can employ the same appropriate problem-solving techniques over time, the problems to be solved and the personnel available to solve them vary greatly.

Three insights can be drawn from developmental theory which help advance our understanding of family crisis. The first is that change is a necessary part of family life.

3

Over the family's life cycle, family personnel changes as people enter as infants and leave as young adults. Cross-generational relationships are revised to reflect this process of maturation. There are other aspects of family life which change over time as well but the ones just mentioned are sufficient to indicate that there is no way that the family can exist over time without dealing with internal change.

This brings us to the second insight. The developmental perspective, seeing family time in terms of broad sweeps, encourages the view that some crises are specific to particular stages and, being specific, they can be anticipated. All new families have to deal with organizational matters which are significant only at the beginning of their relationship. Much later they will have to deal with the reorganization that takes place after the death of a spouse. Between these challenges come other critical situations which are specific to particular stages. Birth, launching, and retirement are just such crises; each is related to a unique developmental stage and each can be seen as being "on the way".

The third insight is that time passes in only one direction- that there can be only one first meeting, one first child, one first death. That being the case, the family must learn new lessons periodically. Families expend scarce energy to learn to do things that they will do only once. The family's problem is to draw lessons from these singular experiences which can be later used with other and different situations.

Even though families must deal with change, to do so is problematic. Problems related to change are better understood with a systems perspective. It is to the consideration of systems that we now turn.

THE FAMILY AS A SYSTEM

A system is a collection of interdependent parts and the relationships that exist between the parts. Systemic interdependency is such that a change in one part tends to change the other parts to some extent and it tends to change the whole. These tendencies will lead to a system change only if the revised activity persists in its new form.

Take the Jones family for example. Their family consists, in part, of an adult woman and an adult man and two children, a boy and a girl. The other part of the system consists of the relationships between the parts, that is, the way they interact with each other and the rules which govern their interaction. Let's say the family is a close one. That is, they know about each other's activities, they interact frequently and deeply, they support each other and

4

expect heavy involvement from each family member. When one of the children wants more independence, he or she will have to draw away from the family group and this action will threaten the family's closeness. Whether the old and close regime will be reaffirmed or whether a new and more loose system will be established is something which depends on such factors as the family's internal strength, the power of the change agent's personality, and external forces which are available to support either side.

Revisions in the family system, such as those required by developmental change, would be rapid and radical were it not that systems reduce the effect of change by means of homeostatic devices. Continuing our example, if Mr. Jones is usually joyful, when he comes home in an angry mood the family will tend to act such that his anger is lessened. The family members want him to become more like his usual self so that they can interact in their accustomed ways. The conserving processes tend to maintain a kind of equilibrium which helps the system to remain integrated and continuous. The drawback of these homeostatic devices is that they make change difficult, this being a drawback when change is necessary for the system's continued well-being.

The idea of homeostasis is central to this inquiry. The idea emerged in the late 1950's when psychiatrists such as Don D. Jackson and R.D. Laing, communications experts such as Jay Haley and Paul Watzlawick, and students of family life such as Ezra Vogel and Norman Bell began to see the family as a system rather than as either a collection of individuals or an adjunct of society. Don D. Jackson[4] was among the earliest of these pioneers and his idea of "homeostasis" is important to the understanding of change-related problems. According to Jackson, families stabilize with a certain internal state, a particular set of dynamic patterns. When this state and these patterns are disturbed, the family attempts to re-establish them and thereby regain homeostasis. Homeostatic devices are those techniques used by the family to regain its former state. More is said about homeostasis in the review found in Chapter 4.

The system has boundaries and intramural interaction is different from transactions between system members and non-members. Sometimes the boundaries are visible: the Jones

---

[4] A compendium of Don D. Jackson's work, along with his co-workers in the "Palo Alto Group", is presented in the book *Communication, Family and Marriage*, Palo Alto, CA: Science and Behavior Books, 1968. An Analysis of Jackson's work and impact is found in G.S. Greenberg, "The Family Interactional Perspective: A Study and Examination of the Work of Don D. Jackson," *Family Process*, 9, 1977, pp. 385-412.

lock their doors and have a fence around their yard.
Sometimes the boundaries are invisible. The Jones have no
friends and they never entertain in their home. The Jones
are an example of a system that is generally closed. Theirs
is a closed system in that its boundaries are well
established and the amount of information which is exchanged
between the family system and other systems is kept to a
minimum. No family system is totally closed. The Jones are
just more closed than others.

At the other end of the scale are open systems and, in
these, there is a more permeable boundary with more
information exchanged. Secrets are fewer and there is a more
general transfer of energy, information, and resources to
and from those outside. The more that is exchanged between a
system and other systems, the more open it is.

Open systems and closed systems are "ideal types" and,
as such, are constructs that do not exist in reality. They
are logical extremes and because they are at opposite ends
of a continuum, they provide a range which allows for
classification. No system is completely closed or perfectly
open; they are only more or less so. Every family has
boundaries that are more or less clear; all boundaries are
permeable to some degree.

Let us consider the Jones family again. Mr. Jones likes
his job and he is usually happy when he comes home at the
end of his work day. One day he comes home in a sour mood.
His behavior triggers, or so it seems, a sequence of events
which result in an angry wife, a tearful daughter, and an
alienated son. The three people look at poor father Jones
and tell him that it is all his fault because he came home
in such an ugly mood. Mr. Jones, on the other hand,
remembers other times when he came home equally depressed,
(note the subtle change in terminology, he sees himself as
depressed they see him as mean) and he was given support and
nurturance by Mrs. Jones. In that former instance, he came
out of it quickly and the deleterious effects of his
depression were not felt. Given his perspective, the problem
is not his depression but the definition of that depression
as meanness and the ensuing effects of the self-fulfilling
prophecy. Which analysis is correct? Both are partially
correct and partially wrong. The most correct answer is that
the source of the problem exists in the family system's
dynamics at that particular time. Since husband and wife
and, to a lesser extent, the children were participating in
the system, they all contributed to the disagreeable
situation.

There are two points to this. First, in the systems
perspective "cause and effect" relationships are circular
not linear. While it is true that A's behavior affects B's,
this is a limited view because A's behavior took place in a
context which was at least partially created by B. So, A's

6

"original" behavior was affected by B's presence and prior behavior. Of course, B's behavior in setting the scene is influenced by A and the whole process can go backward in infinite regression. In interaction processes, there is no beginning, no end, neither cause nor effect.[5]

The other point is that it is inadequate to view the behavior of either A or B in isolation. Behavior in families is not the result of individual personality as much as it is the result of a particular mix of personalities. To understand the behavior of family member A and family member B, the unit of interaction, AB, must be the focus. AB includes the mix of A's and B's perceptions of that which occurred previously, the particular meshing of their goals, and the particular combination of their mental, physical and emotional states. The unique way that A and B merge is something that must be considered in itself. The union AB is not understandable by knowing all about either A or B for the unit AB is greater than the sum of its parts. Characteristics emerge which can not be found in either one or the other but are the result of the interaction mix.

You can see this emergent quality of groups by considering your own experience. Think about the interaction that results when you are with one of your parents and when you are with one of your friends. The difference in the style of interaction can not be traced to you for you are involved in both situations. It can not be traced to the parent or friend for they too are involved in groups with different styles. It must be, then, that the stylistic differences are to be found, not in the parts, but in the unique combination of the parts. In various groups, different facets of personality are emphasized. Since we both act and react, over time, we affect others in their particular accentuation of us. The result is that as the group continues over time its style becomes less and less traceable to the individuals involved; more and more, the group becomes its own best explanation.

The systems perspective enables us to look at persistence and helps us to understand why families have difficulty in changing. Change is difficult because one family member cannot bring about the revision of patterns

---

[5] It might be assumed that this infinite regression ceases sometime and that when A meets B for the first time there is initial action and reaction. For better or worse, this is not the case because one's appearance provides a context: one's age, one's sex, one's voice, one's smell, one's physical closeness, etc. Moreover, the resulting interaction is based on preconceptions supplied by society and the participants' unique experience.

7

unless other members are willing to revise their behavior. These others may not wish to change, a common situation, or they may respond in ways which the changer did not anticipate. In either case, there are restraints placed on a system component by other parts of the system.

There is another side of persistence and the inter-relatedness of a system's components. Any time that one part of a system changes, there will be changes elsewhere in the system. Either the rest of the system changes to accomodate the new behavior or the rest of the system mobilizes its efforts to minimize the effect of the change. In either case, a change in one part of the system will be associated with changes in the other parts.

There is one more insight, a family system involves many different activities. These activities reflect values and goals and the activities, values, and goals form a generally consistent whole. A change in one pattern of behavior means that other activities will be affected. Again, the whole family system must respond if any change is to be made.

Family change is either of the first or second order variety.[6] Second order change is drastic change and the family that emerges from this change is different from the family that existed before. There may be a change in its personnel, in its rules, in its functions, in its organization, or in all these elements. With this kind of change the old family system is gone and can never again be regained. A new system lives and with it is a new family structure with new patterns of interaction.

First order change is milder in that the family revises its patterns in order to maintain the family system rather than to revise it. For example, a husband will change his behavior from remote to close if he feels that his wife is loosening her family bonds to a dangerous degree. His change and her reaction can be seen as a first order family change in that the immediate interaction patterns have been revised in order that the long-term level of closeness is maintained. Homeostatic devices are associated with first order change for they support the status quo.

The concept that there are different kinds of change is both difficult to comprehend and basic to the understanding of family crisis. The fact that it is basic suggests that it be considered now. Its complexity, however, requires that it be discussed later. Since everything can not be done at once, I will wait on this. First we will consider some

---

[6] Paul Watzlawick, John H. Weakland and Richard Fisch, Change (New York: Norton, 1974), pp. 1-28.

aspects of the crisis process and hint at different kinds of change. Later, in the last part of Chapter 4, first and second order change will be considered in depth.

NINE BASIC IDEAS

The systems perspective and the developmental framework provide nine ideas which form the basis for this model. These ideas are:

1. The family is a number of people in interaction who consider themselves to be family members and different from those who are non-family.

2. The family is largely an open system in that it is affected by what takes place elsewhere in the larger social system.

3. A change in the family as a whole will change all parts of the family, a change in one part will tend to bring about a change in all parts.

4. The family's internal dynamics are the result of the particular family mix, no one person is the cause of any other person's behavior for all generate the social context in which each person's behavior makes sense.

5. The family develops patterns of behavior over time and these patterns involve the interdependent family members in task related and integrative activities.

6. Inconstancy in persons, families, and society is a fact of life. A family's continued ability to fulfill its instrumental and integrative requirements will necessitate the revision of its patterns so that they appropriately reflect each altered situation.

7. Patterns are difficult to change as family members try to retain patterns with which they are comfortable. The person who is dissatisfied in a family of satisfied people will find it difficult to generate change.

8. Problems which result from the necessity to change and the reluctance to do so are eventually resolved by the family's separation, the destruction of an individual, or the family's growth. All three of these involve confusion and may be associated with

9

pain. A fourth alternative, the family's continued struggling without resolution of its difficulties, is also possible.

9. Although dealing with crisis is difficult for families, it also has a brighter side. It is through the crisis experience that a family learns about itself. Through crisis, a family changes and moves to different and more appropriate patterns of behavior; a crisis is an opportunity for a family to build a satisfying future.

The model which is explored and presented in this book is based on these nine ideas.

FAMILY CRISIS: DEFINITION

Family crisis has been defined in many different ways[7]

---

[7] Glasser and Glasser say that "A crisis exists when some stressor or event produces stress or disequilibrium for the unit under discussion." (p. 6) Also, "All forms of abrupt or disjunctive changes are likely to cause crisis." Paul H. Glasser and Lois N. Glasser, Families in Crisis (New York: Harper & Row, 1970). "A crisis is any decisive change which creates a situation for which the habitual behavior patterns of a person or a group are inadequate." So say Ernest W. Burgess, Harvey J. Locke and Mary Margaret Thomes. The Family (New York: Van Nostrand, 1971), p. 501. "...A crisis is an event which strains the resources which families possess, cannot be solved by the repertory of ready-made answers provided by the mores or built up out of the family's previous experience with trouble, and requires the family to find new (and usually expedient) ways of carrying on family operations." Willard Waller and Reuben Hill, The Family (New York: Holt, Rinehart and Winston, 1951), p. 456. Farber defines crisis as a situation "which induces a process in family life which is counter to the ordinary organization of the norms and values of the family members." Farber, op. cit., p. 392. A recent definition is, "...any situation which the participants of a social system recognize as being a threat to the status quo, well-being or survival of the system or any of its parts, whose ordinary coping mechanisms and resources are stressed or inadequate for meeting the threat." Jean Lipman-Blumen, "A Crisis Framework applied to Macrosociological Family Changes: Marriage, Divorce, and Occupational Trends Associated with World War II," Journal of Marriage and the Family, 37, 1975, pp. 889-902.

for the subject is both fascinating and complex and researchers tend to emphasize one of its many aspects. Despite the many views of family crisis, most definitions include the idea that a crisis occurs when a family is forced by a stressor to make a change in its established patterns. The model presented in this book uses that general statement and defines family crisis as a process which begins with an inappropriate pattern and ends with the family's reorganization as either intact or modified. An inappropriate pattern is one that does not accomplish what it is supposed to accomplish or it accomplishes its intent but does so in ways that weaken other parts of family life.

A recent review of crisis literature[1] indicates an emerging consensus regarding the meaning of crisis-related terms and the terminology in this model generally harmonizes with the consensus. Drawing on Hill, this review defines stressors as "life events or occurrences of sufficient magnitude to bring about a change in the family system." "Stress" refers to the family's unmanaged tensions that the stressor has generated. "Crisis" refers to family disorganization or "incapacitatedness" in situations in which resources are insufficient. My conceptualization is in line with this consensus if crisis is seen as a process involving inadequate resources that exist <u>before</u> the stressor as well as after. A major point of my model is that it often is the family's inadequacy which serves to bring about the stressor event.

· Defining crisis as I have gives it four components. First, the crisis situation includes a period of time when the inappropriate pattern exists and its inappropriateness is not corrected by the family. This is the Period of Incipience. Secondly, the crisis situation includes a Stressor event which forces family members to be aware that family well-being requires the correction of the inappropriate pattern. Thirdly, crisis includes the family's struggle to find a more appropriate pattern. This is the Secondary Adjustment Period. The fourth part of the crisis process is Reorganization. During Reorganization the family restructures itself so that the newly established appropriate pattern is compatible with other parts of the family's organization. Since success is problematic, that is, since not all can reorganize as viable and intact families, this model also refers to the family's transformation with the separation of its adult members. "Transformation" is used rather than "dissolution" because the latter implies a total and general destruction of the relationship. Since that complete a break occurs only

---

[1] Hamilton J. McCubbin, <u>et al</u>. "Family Stress and Coping: A Decade Review," <u>Journal of Marriage and the Family</u>, 42, 1980, pp. 855-872.

rarely, "transformation", with its emphasis on change and structural difference, seems more fitting.

AN OVERVIEW

Figure I which follows on the next page is a graphic representation of the crisis process and the four parts of this process (Incipience, Stressor, Secondary Adjustment, Reorganization) are clearly indicated. The remainder of the book is an exploration of the model's theory but, before getting into the details, an overview of the model is called for and is presented on the next pages.

The Period of Incipience

If you look at Figure I, you can see that there are two ways that families enter the crisis process. Some families are functioning perfectly well but are swept into the crisis process by some unusual circumstance for which they are unprepared. The accidental death of a young child is an example. The second way into crisis is taken by families whose patterns are dysfunctional to the extent that they are incapable of withstanding either an unusual stressor or ordinary to-be-expected difficulties.

Families of the second kind, chronically dysfunctional ones, are characterized by the existence of some inappropriateness which the family has failed to correct. The family not only fails to rectify this inappropriateness, it sustains it by making compensating changes in related patterns. In this way, the family avoids immediate change but only puts off the day of reckoning for, sooner or later, the inappropriateness will come back to haunt it. A family may not be aware of its inappropriateness or its efforts to avoid change; family members only wish to avoid the uncertainty and stress which accompany the development and incorporation of new patterns.

The Stressor

A stressor is some particular event which indicates pattern inappropriateness to at least one family member. Stressors may have their source either within the family (the first child's birth) or outside (breadwinner's job loss); they may be widespread, affecting many families in a time or place (war) or singular (a death). Stressors are classified as either predictable (retirement) or unpredictable (an automobile accident) depending on whether or not the stressor could be anticipated.

The stressor is some event that occurs to which the family reacts and reaction begins with a definition. The accuracy of the definition as to the stressor's importance and impact directly relates to the family's success in

12

I.Period of Incipience

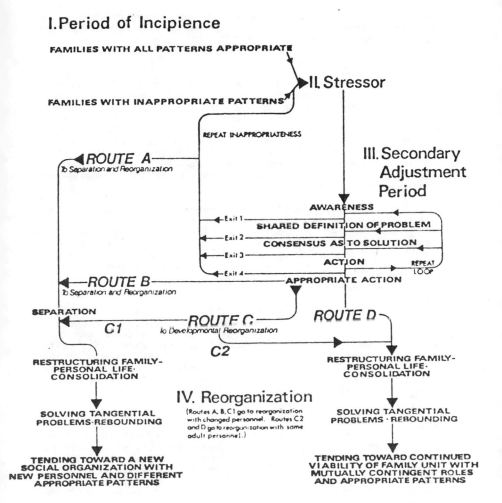

FAMILIES WITH ALL PATTERNS APPROPRIATE

II. Stressor

FAMILIES WITH INAPPROPRIATE PATTERNS

REPEAT INAPPROPRIATENESS

ROUTE A
To Separation and Reorganization

III. Secondary Adjustment Period

AWARENESS
← Exit 1   SHARED DEFINITION OF PROBLEM
← Exit 2   CONSENSUS AS TO SOLUTION
← Exit 3   ACTION   REPEAT LOOP
← Exit 4   APPROPRIATE ACTION

ROUTE B
To Separation and Reorganization

SEPARATION
C1   *ROUTE C*
          To Developmental Reorganization   *ROUTE D*
C2

RESTRUCTURING FAMILY·
PERSONAL LIFE·
CONSOLIDATION

RESTRUCTURING FAMILY·
PERSONAL LIFE·
CONSOLIDATION

IV. Reorganization
(Routes A, B, C1 go to reorganization
with changed personnel. Routes C2
and D go to reorganization with some
adult personnel.)

SOLVING TANGENTIAL
PROBLEMS·REBOUNDING

SOLVING TANGENTIAL
PROBLEMS · REBOUNDING

TENDING TOWARD A NEW
SOCIAL ORGANIZATION WITH
NEW PERSONNEL AND DIFFERENT
APPROPRIATE PATTERNS

TENDING TOWARD CONTINUED
VIABILITY OF FAMILY UNIT WITH
MUTUALLY CONTINGENT ROLES
AND APPROPRIATE PATTERNS

Figure I   GRAPHIC MODEL OF FAMILY CRISIS

response. Response takes place during the next stage, the Secondary Adjustment Period, and it is to processes related to that stage that we now turn.

The Secondary Adjustment Period

During this period, the family's task is to replace their inappropriate patterns with new and appropriate ones. This replacement takes place in five steps which have certain success-enhancing characteristics. Chances for success are improved if the family moves quickly to identify the difficulty and correct it. The longer the family delays correction, the more disruption there is in the family and the less energy will be available for pattern revision. Also, slow progress and/or repeated failure negatively affect group morale.

The family must also balance instrumental and integrative functions. If the former predominates, revision will be marked by authority and discipline and, if excessive, the contemporary family's raison d'etre, fulfillment of intimacy, authenticity, whole-person needs, will be lost. A one-sided emphasis on integration, on the other hand, will not supply the stiffness and direction that is necessary for corrective activity.

So too, it is necessary for flexibility and consistency to be balanced. Creative flexibility is obviously necessary; consistency is required if the family is to retain some sense of itself as a continuing identifiable unit with certain values. Pattern revision is most likely if the family moves through the five steps quickly while maintaining a balance between flexibility and continuity; between instrumentality and integration.

The process of pattern revision involves a series of steps. Awareness can come to one family member but successful correction requires the concerted effort of many family members. The steps in the Secondary Adjustment Period concern the activity associated with turning an individual's perception into group action. The family must first share awareness of the problem. This leads to a definition of the problem or identification of the inappropriate pattern. The third step is to reach consensus as to solution and this is followed by the family's agreement on appropriate remedial action. Finally, corrective action completes the process.

As shown in Figure I, the family may move systematically through each of these steps directly to the point where they take appropriate action. This action can lead them in several directions. Route D has them restructuring themselves, usually with the same family membership and always with the same members of the older generation. Route C takes families to Reorganization with a personnel change, C1 families having lost one of the older

14

generation and C2 families having lost one of the younger members. Husbands and wives on Route B have decided that their most appropriate action is to go separate ways and this is appropriate for them as the decision is conscious and responsibility for it is fully assumed.

Other families do not make it to the appropriate action step. These unfortunate (incompetent?) ones take an "exit" and either go back to a pre-stressor situation and continue in their inappropriate ways and await another stressor or they take Route A to separation. This separation is different from that associated with Route B as Route A separation is characterized by an inability to resolve the problem in a constructive manner.

More fortunate families have encountered some temporary difficulty during Secondary Adjustment and take a "repeat loop" by which they correct their previous action or interpretation. They can then move toward Reorganization without the impetus of another stressor.

Reorganization

At this point in the crisis process, major change has occurred within the family system. It remains for the family to make the necessary system adjustments to incorporate the newly developed pattern and to move a to a new dynamic equilibrium. There exists two tasks: consolidating and rebounding. In consolidation, the focus is on achieving pattern consistency within the system. Associated behaviors which support the new pattern must be developed to replace behaviors which compensated for earlier inappropriateness. In rebounding, the focus is on family members' needs. Needs are poorly served during earlier stages of crisis because energies are directed toward solving immediate and difficult problems. Family members' enjoyment of each other, their spontaneous as well as their predictable interaction, their integration and instrumentality may have all suffered during the crisis period and the family's continued health requires their re-establishment.

Concluding Thoughts

This, then, has been a brief overview of the model of family crisis. The model provides an account of the ways that families deal with their need to change and their resistance to do so. The model provides an outline of the process whereby families move through crisis and cope with it, emerging as stronger units, either intact or modified. On the other hand, it specifies the processes associated with the family's transformation; the result of its inability to correct dysfunction. It helps to explain the dynamics of families of a third type, those who continue to limp along. Finally, the model promotes the consideration of crisis as both a challenge and a travail for it has

15

sufficient scope to embrace developmental and idiosyncratic crises and to specify their effect on functional and dysfunctional families.

Time is an important element in this model; the crisis process is seen as a series of steps. The steps are sequential to each other and, yet, within each step, behavior is interactional and therefore subject to a different kind of process. I am saying that the interaction at any particular step is interrelated, mutually impinging, and circular and we can talk of it using such terms as "related" and "associated with". These terms preclude any temporal ordering and point to essential interrelatedness. On the other hand, the temporal nature of the step sequence is linear because time, practically speaking, moves forward only and certain events occur prior to others. Different words apply to the series of steps; words such as "source", "bring about" and "cause" are used. These words indicate the effect of some prior event on that which follows. Both the circular and the linear perspective are helpful in understanding family crisis and they give the most assistance when they are differentiated and applied where relevant.

To summarize, in this chapter we have seen how this model of family crisis incorporates insights from the developmental framework to explain why families must deal with change. These insights help show that there is no way that crisis can be avoided. General systems theory was used to support the model in areas related to the family's difficulty in changing. From the developmental framework and general systems theory a set of nine ideas was developed and the model was described as an extension of these basic ideas.

Family crisis was then defined as the situation associated with the family's necessity to change its patterns, this necessity being indicated by some stressor event. This definition suggests a four step progression which takes families from an original set of patterns, through the two periods when they experience a stressor and make remedial effort, and concludes with the family's development of new and effective patterns. We now will move to Chapter 2, the first of the chapters concerned with a more detailed examination of the crisis process.

16

CHAPTER 2

THE PERIOD OF INCIPIENCE

In this, the first part of the crisis process, our focus is on the way that families generate a crisis for themselves: how their inappropriate patterns develop and are left uncorrected; how the families move toward the Stressor. We will see how patterns become inappropriate, why they are not changed, and we will find out about the benefits and costs of maintaining an internal consistency which includes a non-workable pattern. There are a number of definitional matters which will be taken up as we progress.

The aim of the first part of the chapter is to indicate the nature of patterns, that is, to explore their redundancy, impermanence, inertia, and function. This is done so that, in the last part of the chapter, families can be categorized. The categorization stems from the idea that families have different kinds of difficulties, these difficulties being a function of their particular type of inadequacy. The categorization specifies types of families as these types are generated by the family's kind of inadequacy. I believe that understanding is advanced by the initial consideration of patterns, the subsequent specification of the inadequacies, and the corresponding classification of families.

PATTERNS

Persistence

As Joan Jackson wrote, "When persons live together over a period of time, patterns evolve of relating to one another and behaving as a unit."[1] She is saying that interaction becomes repetitious and this repetitiveness gives to behavior a pattern. The family's patterns are its accepted and expected ways of behaving.

Patterned behavior is highly predictable in that it occurs in sequences which are known to family members. Usually, family members can tell who will be performing certain tasks. Think of your own family and pick some day next week. Who will be doing the cooking? working to bring in money? relieving family tension with humor? starting an argument? getting hooked into the argument? making

---

[1] Joan K. Jackson, "The Adjustment of the Family to Alcoholism," *Marriage and Family Living*, 18, 1956, p. 361.

decisions? criticising these decisions? Who in your family escalates conflict and who backs off to avoid a continued or increasingly bitter interchange? The point is that the family has unique ways of accomplishing its requirements and these are repeated and become well established. Being set, the behavioral sequences can be predicted. It is the "here we go again" phenomenon, the awareness of virtually every family member that a familiar sequence has begun.

Patterns are associated with all manner of family activity. There are role performance patterns, patterns associated with the content and manner of interaction, and patterns associated with the division of labor and decision making. Patterns also involve action not taken. In short, patterns are the family's customary way of handling their affairs.

During the Period of Incipience, patterns become potentially destructive because of their inadequacy. That is, they do not accomplish that which they were meant to accomplish in ways that support family viability. This inadequacy is called "inappropriateness". It is during the Period of Incipience that pattern inappropriateness commences. This inadequacy may not be known to the family or it may be known but not corrected. With no correction, the family moves toward the time when a stressor will force the family to be aware of the problem.

Vogel and Bell[2] indicate in their brilliant article an excellent example of such inappropriateness. They found that families with an emotionally disturbed child had unresolved stress-creating difficulties in the family system and they stated that the child's emotional disturbance was used, even created, to lessen the damaging effects of the continuing stress. This scapegoating is inappropriate because, although it provides tension release, it diverts the parents' attention from the source of the problem and correction is rendered impossible. Eventually, the uncorrected problem and/or the related complications bring about a stressor.

At this stage in the development of the model, the important point is that inappropriate patterns exist during Incipience and sometimes they are corrected and sometimes they are not. In the former situation, the crisis process is halted. In the latter, a Stressor will eventually introduce another stage of the crisis process.

---

[2] Ezra F. Bell and Norman W. Bell, "The Emotionally Disturbed Child as a Family Scapegoat," The Family, (eds.) N.W. Bell and E.F. Vogel (Glencoe: The Free Press, 1960), pp. 382-397.

18

Change

Why do patterns become inappropriate? Why are these inadequate patterns not corrected? Because the existence of the uncorrected and inappropriate pattern is at the heart of family crisis, the answers to these two questions are vital to our inquiry. The issue can be seen as a paradox in that on the one hand, patterns are difficult to change and, on the other hand, family well-being requires that these patterns **must** be changed. We will explore the issue and consider first why patterns are difficult to revise.

Patterns: difficult to change. The first reason why patterns are difficult to change is that current patterns are the family's first choice. Of all available alternatives, the family has consciously or unconsciously chosen a particular one. To change is to move to another pattern which was previously defined as not as good. Obviously, people would rather stick with their first choice than discard it for something they have perceived as being less valuable.

To move away from tried and comfortable patterns is to move toward ones that are new and untried. There is risk-taking involved and as Thomas Jefferson said in the American Declaration of Independence, "...all experience hath shown that mankind are more disposed to suffer while evils are sufferable, than to right themselves by abolishing the forms to which they are accustomed." For families as with nations, risk taking is not easy for it entails a rethinking of one's present, a reorganization of one's biography, and a reordering of one's aspirations.

Moreover, the implementation of any new idea is inefficient and this inefficiency represents a loss when compared to the practised and efficient pattern that is being replaced. This immediate loss is certain while the compensating long term gain is less sure. There must be a leap of faith if a person is to invest in some glorious but indefinite future with currency taken from a present which may have precious little to give. As Gregory Bateson put it, "All we need to be sure of is that, at any moment, achievement is just around the corner."[3] This optimism is difficult in a family that is falling apart.

Another reason why change is difficult is that family members invest heavily in their patterns. If the patterns result from a concerted and conscious effort, there will likely be a heavy emotional investment. More frequently, patterns are the product of drift and, because the drift is

---

[3]   Gregory Bateson, Steps to an Ecology of Mind (New York: Ballantine Books, 1972), p. 176.

19

gradual and the direction vague, the family members behave unconsciously and automatically. Because the patterns are part of a rarely questioned world-taken-for-granted, they continue indefinitely and unchanged.

Parenting provides us with examples of inappropriate patterns which result from conscious effort and inappropriateness which arises from gradual drift. The former is exemplified by the parent who prides himself on consistency. He perceives himself to be a good parent and sees his consistency as a part of that goodness. His decisions are made on the basis of their congruency with past parental behavior. Change is difficult for this parent because change means inconsistency and he has defined inconsistency as unacceptable. This father has a son and, as the two age, their relative positions change accordingly. The father's emphasis on consistency will lead to parenting problems for his expectations will be based on his recollection of the past as that recollection is molded by the compulsion for consistency.

And now for gradual drift. Frequently, parenting is unconscious and parental behavior is a reflection of the combination of parents' personality needs and family dynamics. If the parents are dissatisfied with each other as spouses, and if a change is not made, it is likely that the child will slowly be included in the spousal difficulty, "triangulated" is the word, to drain away the pressures that are otherwise unrelieved.[4] Triangulation is gradual because it takes a while for the parents to realize that the child can be used in this way; it takes time for the exploitive patterns to be established and the child does not immediately adapt to the pain which is engendered by triangulation. The parental maneuver is unplanned and the process is made up as it goes along and, in that sense, people drift into it. Whether by drift or conscious effort, family members become involved in patterned behavior which, by virtue of its perceived desirability, its efficiency, and members' high degree of comfort with the associated roles, is difficult to revise.

Patterns: the necessity to change. Even though it is difficult for families to change their patterns, this change is required. Change in contemporary society, in its culture and institutions, engenders change in the family. But even if there were no cultural change, families would need to develop new patterns because of changes in family personnel, changes brought about by ageing, and because of inconstancy in family members' relative positions. These are family universals and are independent of any particular social

---

[4]   Minuchin, op. cit., p. 9, 101-105; Lederer and Jackson, op. cit., p. 14; Vogel and Bell, op. cit.

setting.

The necessity of change and the family's inertia are at the center of the crisis process. Family crisis can be seen as the process associated with the family's revision of the patterns which weaken it. The crisis process includes the formation of these inappropriate patterns, the stressor which forces the inappropriateness into the consciousness of the family members, the efforts of the family to establish new and appropriate patterns, and the reorganizing of the family structure around these new patterns. Although it is usually a gradual drift which creates the problem of inappropriateness, a concerted effort involving complex dynamics is necessary if correction is to take place. It is the problem of pattern inappropriateness and family inertia that we will explore with this model.

Patterns: the ability to change. In concluding this section on pattern persistence and change, a word of caution must be expressed here or else a distorted view of family life might result. Families are not only reacting agents, they are actors in a social context. Moreover, families do not only strive to maintain stability, they sometimes opt for growth and resultant instability. Although it is generally true that families resist change until it is forced on them, it is also true that families process information that comes from inside and outside. In its information handling, a family may change its behavior to make it agree with its goals and it may even change its basic values and the related behavior. This change is an act of choice.

If a family has goals and these goals are kept in mind, a family will process information coming to it and can revise its patterns of its own volition. For example, a family which sets out to assist each member to accomplish some task may well experiment with different interaction and transaction patterns to see which will be most helpful. In their experimentation, there will be risk taking, rational thinking, and a reluctance to invest heavily in any pattern until it has proven value. Blessed are such families, for they will accomplish reasonable objectives.

To this point in the development of the model, we have discussed the persistence of a family's patterns and the need for pattern revision. We have seen that changes in either the social setting or the family's internal arrangement can confound its smooth operation in that its once appropriate patterns no longer work. The idea of pattern appropriateness and inappropriateness is important to this model and will now be considered in depth.

21

Appropriate Patterns, Inappropriate Patterns

Patterns are either appropriate or inappropriate, appropriate patterns being those that can be continued indefinitely. If the characteristics of family members, the family, and its social setting were somehow to remain constant, appropriate patterns would be those which could be continued over time with the family unit remaining intact and viable. Appropriate patterns enable the family to meet the expectations of society, to satisfy the needs of individual family members, and to satisfy family structural requirements. One example of an appropriate pattern is the family's handling of finances such that income exceeds expenses.

Appropriateness and inappropriateness become very complicated when a pattern appears to be appropriate at one level (at the level of family interaction, for example) and inappropriate at another (at the person level). To refer to a previous example, the scapegoating of a child may appear to be appropriate for the family as it provides tension release and promotes integration. Yet it is inappropriate at the individual level for the child's growth and well-being are restricted. Since families as well as theoreticians and therapists have great difficulty in sorting out such situations, the matter deserves careful consideration which it will now get.

Unless personal well-being and family unity are advanced simultaneously, a pattern is considered to be inappropriate. Such a pattern cannot be continued indefinitely for several reasons. In the first place, this pattern indirectly affects family interaction because it generates resentment. This resentment results in overt or covert behavior by which a person enhances himself at the family's expense. Patterns associated with generating or exercising this sort of self enhancement are inappropriate because they will eventually create great stress as each family member strives to get their "just desserts".

Moreover, a pattern which purchases family unity with personal damage is <u>directly</u> inappropriate because (1) the gains in unity are only short term, (2) the major problem is not solved and will result in further stress, and (3) the damage to the individual will create additional problems which will weaken the family. Appropriateness must apply at both the family and personal level or the family is heading into crisis.

Even if appropriateness exists at all levels, it is usually temporary as most patterns do not maintain their effectiveness indefinitely. Since neither the family's characteristics nor its social setting remains fixed, appropriate patterns become inappropriate. The inappropriateness can be evident at any of the three levels.

22

That is, it is manifest if a family member's mental and physical well-being is reduced, if the family is unable to meet its social obligations, or if the family's own organizational requirements are unfulfilled. If any of the inappropriate patterns are structurally vital and never corrected, their inappropriateness will result in the family's dissolution. If inappropriate, uncorrected, and not particularly vital, the inappropriateness will result in the unpleasantness of unresolvable conflict.

So, patterns are appropriate or inappropriate; appropriateness must exist at all levels and is usually temporary. Next is another classification of patterns which is based, not on how well they work, but on what it is that they are intended to do. That is, some, called execution patterns, aim at accomplishing the family's day to day business and others, called correction patterns, attempt to straighten out difficulty when the execution patterns fail to work effectively. We will now look more closely.

Execution and Correction Patterns

The classification of patterns on the basis of what they do is helpful in furthering the understanding of families in crisis. Usually, families are in crisis situations because of some failing in an execution pattern. Bills may not be paid. A child may not be attending school. A house may be falling down. These are three examples of ineffective execution patterns which are about to bring on a stressor or have already done so. These are the "immediate" difficulties to which attention must be directed. At the same time, these immediate difficulties usually exist because patterns have not been properly revised. So, the conclusion follows that a stressor indicates ineffectiveness in correction patterns. Therefore, to help a family, it is necessary to consider its problems with both execution and correction patterns and to maintain the distinction between the two.

These ideas will be explored in the following pages. I will begin with a brief definition of each type of pattern and then discuss the differences in detail.

Execution patterns. Patterns whose objective is the performance of a task are called execution patterns. They are associated with getting some specific thing accomplished. These patterns include such essential activities as purchasing food, making love, and obtaining housing. They also include less important activities, those dealing with the essential trivia of daily life.

There is no way that all of a family's execution patterns can remain appropriate for long periods of time. These patterns require revision if the family is to continue to be strong; revision is accomplished by means of

23

correction patterns.

Correction patterns. These are so called because of their particular importance in the revision of inappropriate execution patterns. An example might be helpful. If a family had a particular money spending pattern (an execution pattern) which was no longer appropriate because of a substantial and non-remedial decrease in income, a new spending pattern would be necessitated. The related correction pattern might include a discussion and a compromise and a decision. These steps would comprise the correction pattern and would lead to change in the family's execution patterns related to their spending money. The manner in which the family establishes this new execution pattern is their correction pattern. Correction patterns are concerned with remedy, with adjustment, with process. In terms of decision making, correction patterns are related to the process whereby a decision is reached rather than the decision itself.

Differences specified. Execution and correction patterns differ in that execution patterns are specifically related to a particular activity, while correction patterns are more general. The way by which a childless couple meets the need for sexual intimacy and gratification reflects its situation of privacy, convenience, and freedom. The execution pattern associated with sexual activity will have to be corrected when a child is born and the setting is changed by the presence of a demanding third person. The remedial correction pattern, being more general, can be one that was used before and the same pattern of problem solving can be used in subsequent and diverse situations. It is this generality that gives correction patterns their importance.

Correction patterns differ from the execution patterns in that appropriate correction patterns will not need revision. For example, when a couple discovers that a particular balance between honesty and illusion allows them to deal successfully with conflict, it is possible that they have made a discovery that will serve them well for many years. At times, however, previously appropriate correction patterns become inappropriate. When this is the case, remedial activity requires that correction patterns at a different level be employed.

There is one other difference between correction and execution patterns. Execution patterns can be either interactional or transactional; that is, they can be associated with internal affairs or external matters. Correction patterns are only interactional.

To clarify this, terminology, let us consider the purchase and use of an automobile. The actual car purchase is a transactional execution pattern because outsiders become involved. Interactional execution patterns are

24

employed as the choice of make and model is made and
expenditures are adjusted. Later, other interactional
patterns are exercised when the family uses the car and pays
for it. When it is necessary to revise these execution
patterns, as when a stupid purchase has been made or the car
is deteriorating because of inadequate care, correction
patterns are employed.

To summarize, in the foregoing material we have
considered the nature of patterns. We have noted that some
work well, at least temporarily, but most become
inappropriate over time and this inadequacy engenders a
stressor. We have considered why pattern change is necessary
and why families have difficulty in revising their ways.
Finally, we have thought about two different kinds of
patterns, execution and correction, and indicated how they
differ. These insights should have helped us to clarify the
nature of pattern effectiveness and family resistance to
change. Next, we will briefly consider how some families
avoid stressors and then consider other families who do not
make correction during Incipience.

PATTERN CORRECTION DURING INCIPIENCE

During the Period of Incipience, pattern inadequacy
exists. If left uncorrected, the family is moved toward
Stressor, Secondary Adjustment, and Reorganization. If
corrected, and some families do correct their inappropriate
patterns during Incipience, the Stressor and other parts of
the crisis process are avoided. A family needs to be
skillful to make revisions before the situation becomes
critical. Some family member must perceive a pattern's
inappropriateness and other family members must recognize
the value of this perception. Those with power in the family
must recognize that a crisis is on the way and that
something should be done. They must then take corrective
action. Few families are so skillful.

The steps just outlined are the same that a family goes
through during the Secondary Adjustment Period. The steps
are the same but the problems are different. Before the
stressor occurs, the family has difficulty in perceiving the
problem for, during Incipience, pattern inappropriateness is
not sufficiently damaging to be obvious. If perceived by one
person, there is difficulty in getting others to accept the
definition. After the stressor takes place, the problem is
more clear but urgency is a complicating factor. During
Secondary Adjustment, finding a solution is difficult
because of: (1) the great pressure for immediate remedy, (2)
the family's disorganized state, and (3) the possibility of
felt inadequacy and acrimony. More will be said in Chapter 4
about the problems surrounding correction after the
stressor.

25

It would appear that a choice presents itself. Families can either make minor adjustments and experience relatively minor tension and conflict or they can select a policy of non-change and the resulting temporary stability and peace. Of course, this peace will very likely be purchased by greater difficulties further down the line. Our inquiry will now centre on those families who have purchased these greater difficulties.

Routes Through Incipience

Families move through the Period of Incipience toward the stressor by various routes. The routes differ because of variation in family capabilities and differences in kinds of stressors. Later,[5] the impact of the type of stressor will be considered; presently, we will focus on the family's capabilities. Family capability depends on the effectiveness of its patterns. Figure II is a classification of families as to the relative effectiveness of their execution and correction patterns. Families in each of the four categories move through the Period of Incipience in different ways.

A classification of families. First, consider families whose correction patterns and execution patterns are appropriate, those families in Cell #1. It is possible that these families will go long periods without experiencing a stressor. They leave the crisis process early because of the effectiveness of their execution patterns and the strength of their correction patterns. If their execution patterns become ineffective, their strong correction patterns are employed and essential minor adjustments are made before a stressor forces major reorganization. Execution patterns are never allowed to get to the point of prolonged and severe inappropriateness.

For these families to stay free from crisis, they must be lucky as well as wise. Families in Cell #1 that are involved in crisis are carried into the Secondary Adjustment

---

[5]   See Chapter 3 for a complete consideration of different kinds of stressors. What can be said here is that the effect of one kind of crisis (death of a young husband, for example) differs greatly from the effect of another type of crisis (the retirement of a family wage earner). The former type is called "random" or "unpredictable", the latter, "predictable". Predictable stressors are associated with normative life events, those events that are associated with common development-related changes that virtually all families experience. Non-normative events are unique to some families, the other families being fortunate enough to escape them. These non-normative situations are brought to the family by unpredictable stressors.

FIGURE II

CLASSIFICATION OF FAMILIES BY PATTERNS

		CORRECTION PATTERNS	
		APPROPRIATE	INAPPROPRIATE
EXECUTION PATTERNS	APPROPRIATE	1	2
	INAPPROPRIATE	3	4

Period by an unpredictable stressor. Since this stressor event occurs without warning, the family does not have the opportunity to use its strength to prevent it. The family can, however, use its effective patterns after the stressor event and thereby minimize its effect. Families in Cell #1 have no Period of Incipience.

The families in Cell #2 have appropriate execution patterns and inappropriate correction patterns. Their freedom from crisis is usually short-lived for the inevitability of both family change and social change will eventually render inappropriate a formerly appropriate pattern. When this occurs, the inadequacy of their correction patterns will prevent revision and, in time, the family will experience a stressor. The future of these families is bleak for they will have difficulty in revising their patterns after the stressor. They might well remember the "good old days" when, untested, they seemed to be strong and well.

Families with inappropriate execution patterns and appropriate correction patterns, those in Cell #3 are frequently in trouble. The ineffectiveness of their execution patterns keeps them in hot water but they are rescued by the strength of their correction patterns. They remain intact despite their difficulties.

In some ways it is difficult to differentiate Cell #3 families with those in Cell #1. Since both types of families have adequate correction patterns, any ineffectiveness in execution patterns should be temporary for both family types. The difference between the two family types is to be found in the relative quality of the correction patterns.

That is, the correction patterns of Type #3 families are more specific and not as sensitive as those of Type #1. The patterns are not sensitive enough to be employed before a stressor; they cannot deal with pre-stressor sublety to a degree that will allow the early correction that characterizes families in Cell #1. In addition, when families in Cell #1 make a correction, they go more deeply and consider issues at a more basic level. Cell #3 families deal only with the immediate problem.

Understanding of this will be advanced by considering types of change and then an example. Consideration of first and second order change is relevant to Cell #3 families. When inappropriate execution patterns create problems, families can either change their existing behavior and thereby correct the immediate situation (a first order change) or they can correct the inappropriate family way of thinking to which the behavior is related (a second order change). If they make only a first order change, they have merely "bought time" for another problem will emerge. They stay in Cell #3. However, if the family makes a second order change, it is seen as being in Cell #1 for its inappropriate pattern is made appropriate and its correction patterns gain strength.

For example, in the case of over-indebtedness, the immediate situation can be resolved by the borrowing of additional money. Finance companies agreeably offer "payment consolidation" loans and thereby encourage first order change. The immediate problem can also be resolved by a basic change in family thinking. This would not provide relief as rapidly but a repeat of the problem would be less likely. An example of such a second order change would be the reordering of priorities resulting in the lowering of acquisitive aspirations.

My guess is that there are more Type III families than Type I because families seldom make second order changes during Incipience; their efforts are directed toward solving the immediate issues and, what is more important, the underlying difficulty is not even seen. To see the basic problem requires that family members observe something of which they are a part; they must objectify themselves and their family. In order to correct a pattern, the pattern itself and its fit with other family components must be objectively seen. Since these other components include the family members themselves and their interaction, the problem is one of observing oneself and one's most intimate relationships. This is beyond the capacity of most people. As a result, second order change requires either (a) luck, or (b) family members who are able to objectify themselves and their situation and accurately perceive what they have objectified, or (c) the help of a qualified third party, or some combination of the three.

Families are more likely to deal with the immediate problem and leave the basic faulty pattern uncorrected. They are bound to repeat the same pattern and undergo another stressor. Drawing on Koestler, families like these have memories but they do not draw from memories to make correction. "[Their] past...provides no guidance to the future [and]...after each crisis and conciliation, time always starts afresh and history is always in the year zero".[*]

Families in Cell #4 are in trouble. With inadequate execution patterns and with no way to correct them, these families are destined to move toward dissolution.

Family classification and stressor type. The four types of families as indicated by the relative strength of their execution and correction patterns have been specified. This material has been combined with other information, that relating to stressors, and the integration of this is to be found in Figure III and will be used to provide a chapter summary.

In the first column on Figure III, the numbers refer to the cell placement in Figure II. The second column indicates the kinds of patterns which are appropriate for families in any particular cell. Only appropriate patterns are listed, the inappropriate ones can be deduced. In the third column are listed the ways that the families handle change. Finally, in the fourth column are the kinds of stressors which will eventually be felt by the family.

From Figure III, a chapter summary can be developed. Starting with an obvious conclusion; all families are subject to crisis brought about by unpredictable stressors. Since these come without warning and have little or nothing to do with the family's pattern effectiveness, they fall on functional and dysfunctional families alike.

Secondly, family types II, III, and IV experience crises that are associated with predictable events. One important consideration to keep in mind is that the predictable stressor does not "cause" the crisis. It merely exacerbates the previously existing family dysfunction, that which existed during incipience.

---

[*] Arthur Koestler, The Invisible Writing (New York: The Macmillan Company, 1954), p. 218.

FIGURE III

ROUTES THROUGH INCIPIENCE ACCORDING TO
FIGURE II CELL PLACEMENT

Fig II Cell	Approp. Patterns	Method of Handling Change During Incipience	Stressor Type
1	All	Continual revision of execution and correction patterns. No major upheaval.	Unpred.
2	Exec. Only	No problems as long as revision is not needed. Social and family change not met by pattern revision.	Unpred., Pred.
3	Corr. Only	Inappropriate execution patterns corrected after stressor. Families periodically upset.	Unpred., Pred.
4	None	No remedy	Unpred., Pred.

Although all three family types meet with predictable crisis, they do so for different reasons. Type III families undergo crisis because of their inability to handle change in either themselves or in their context. Type II families have difficulty because their correction patterns are not sensitive enough to prevent stressors. Type IV families lose out on all counts for their pattern ineffectiveness brings about numerous difficulties which are not resolvable due to the inappropriateness of their correction patterns.

The needs of each of the four types of families during incipience are different and their chances for success during the crisis process reflect their varying needs. Type I families need very little. Their important need during Incipience is to be aware that 'bad luck may befall them and that, if and when it does, they should not panic but continue to employ the effective patterns that have served them so well in the past.

Type II families will need assistance ("assistance" and "help" as used in this section refer to help that comes from either a family member or someone outside) in improving their correction patterns and, yet this assistance is likely to be accepted only after a stressor event. Until these families are so tested, they will likely believe that they are in good shape and any helper would be hard pressed to achieve consensus that such is not the case. After the stressor they will be more open to suggestions. They will then need short-term help in correcting their immediate

30

execution problem and long term help in correcting their poorly functioning correction pattern. These families have good prospects for success because their experience includes smooth functioning and its related satisfactions.

Type III families can be helped by strengthening their correction patterns so as to make them more sensitive. It may be possible that such help would be rejected for these families might well enjoy the excitement associated with periodic upheaval and the sense of satisfaction that comes from handling such turmoil successfully. The mix of personalities may be such that this is to be valued more than the smooth family operation which characterizes families in Cell #1.

Type IV families have no experience of past success, no satisfaction with the present, no hope for the future. They need all kinds of help but are unlikely to use it because of their dearth of ability and their lack of motivation.

The foregoing has indicated that families move into crisis in a variety of ways, these ways reflecting their strengths and weaknesses in conjunction with the stressor's characteristics. The way the family defines their situation is a good indication of their effective adaptability and we will now consider the definition.

The Definition of the Situation

Before leaving the Period of Incipience, there are two issues requiring clarification and both issues relate to the family's definition that a particular situation is critical. The family's definition is seen as crucial to its success in pattern correction. The first issue concerns the existence and source of the definition and the second concerns its accuracy. These will be taken in order.

In normative crisis,[7] the definition of a situation as critical must follow some inappropriateness. This means that the crisis process includes a time when an inappropriate pattern exists without anyone's knowledge. In saying that, I am making a statement which needs support, for, if no one knows about it, how can it be said to exist? Secondly, who is to say that a family has an inappropriate pattern, the family members or an outside observer? We will briefly consider these two questions.

---

[7] A normative crisis is one that is associated with the family's development. Normative crisis are predictable because virtually all families experience them at some particular stage. Two examples are the first child's birth and the major breadwinner's retirement. Much more is said on this topic in Chapter 3.

31

In answering the first question, one must avoid a trap. It is tautological and too easy to say that we know an inappropriate family pattern exists during Incipience because it later leads to a stressor. The nature of the inquiry supports that kind of retroactive view but, true or not, it is insufficient.

· There are two experientially verifiable perceptions which lead me to believe that pattern inappropriateness exists during Incipience. The first is that in our own families, and in others of which we are so intimate as to be a part, we can think of times in which patterns that were potentially destructive were corrected. I know of a family in which the husband's occupational frustrations led to family conflict. The signs of incipient crisis were all present: unresolved and unacceptable spousal differences existed, neither spouse truly listened to the other and analysis rather than sharing was accentuated. In one dramatic session, matters came to a head and both husband and wife indicated their dissatisfaction with the existing situation. The husband clearly expressed his job related frustrations, the wife shared her insights and feelings. The results were a renewed closeness, additional support for him, more demonstrated care for her, and a better understanding of the importance of dealing with job dissatisfaction at its source. In addition, the couple learned a lesson in problem resolution which could be applied to many different family situations. Of course, this family is not unique; all close and continuing families live this same kind of situation.

In addition to personal experience, family therapy points to the development of inappropriateness during Incipience. Preventative therapy is based on the assumption that faulty patterns can be corrected prior to a stressor and when this therapy is successful, when a stressor is avoided, it supports the idea that inappropriateness exists during Incipience. Therefore, if in our own lives and in families helped by therapy, we know of inappropriateness and correction, I believe it is safe to assume that similar situations exist in other families.

The other question associated with the source of the definition has to do with the family's awareness of the incipient crisis. If a pattern is defined by the observer as inadequate and by the family as adequate, a question that can be raised is, Is the pattern inappropriate or not?

Several possible answers present themselves. One answer is that the family members are the best judge because they are the ones most intimately involved and they should know. Another answer is that the family members, because they are so deeply immersed in the family system, cannot know and that an outside observer is necessary to point out both what they are doing and the long-term effects of their behavior.

The first answer is supported by the fact that families can change and the second answer is supported by the fact that they rarely change their organization without some cataclysmic event. Because family dynamics are so complex and because interaction sequences have consequences which are remote and only subtly related, I believe that family members can behave and not know the implications of their behavior. I believe an outside observer can frequently be the best judge of a pattern's inappropriateness.

A qualification is necessary. Family members are usually the first ones to know that something is wrong. The pain that family members feel when there is hostility, resentment, belittling, and attempts at control is real and there can be no doubt that it is felt by family members who are attuned to their feelings. This pain is a symptom and although it can be effective in motivating change and indicating when change is successfully accomplished, the pain neither indicates what needs to be revised nor the way that revision will be most efficacious. The awareness that a problem exists is not tantamount to the definition that a particular pattern is inappropriate.

The other part of this aside is concerned with the accuracy of the definition. Hill and Hansen[*] indicate that a readiness to define an unusual situation as critical leads to family crisis. As Hill explains it, when a family defines a situation as critical, it over-reacts and this over-reaction produces additional difficulties, secondary problems, which weaken the family structure. For example, sexual responses are affected when the family has exhausted its emotional reserves in dealing with a particular stressor. If that stressor is financially related, sexual responsiveness can be affected by the high level of anxiety and guilt associated with unpaid bills, fear for the future, or a confusion of masculinity with solvency. These secondary problems, in this example sexual dysfunction, then work to create further difficulties.

In Hill and Hansen's work, the emphasis is on the problems created by errors in perception and the resulting definition of non-problems as problems. Although this is undoubtedly true, it is only part of the story. Movement into crisis can also result if a problem is defined as a non-problem and no action is taken. If a pattern is actually inappropriate, to define it as appropriate is just as damaging as the situation to which Hill refers. Problems are formed in three ways: when action is necessary and not taken, when action is taken but is unnecessary and when the

---

[*] Hill, "Generic Features of Families Under Stress," op. cit.; Hansen and Hill, "Families Under Stress," op. cit.

wrong kind of action is taken.[9] Avoiding stressors requires that someone in the family be sensitive to existing and forthcoming problems and the severity of these problems must be correctly assessed. This awareness and assessment is the first step in strengthening the family for, without it, family action will be either non-existent or misplaced.

This completes the consideration of the Period of Incipience. It is during this period that a family problem, left uncorrected, grows. As it grows, other patterns become inappropriate because family patterns tend to reflect each other. Eventually, a stressor occurs because of this inadequate family functioning.

FAMILY STRENGTHS

As I stated earlier, each chapter will end with a summary statement which indicates the family's strengths which help it to successfully meet the challenges associated with the stage of crisis being considered. Following is a list of these strengths as indicated by the model. A family's success in making correction during the Period of Incipience and thereby avoiding a stressor is related to:

1.   The effectiveness of its execution patterns.

2.   The effectiveness of its correction patterns. This effectiveness is related to:

   A.   The awareness of at least one family member that pattern change is necessary.

   B.   The power that the aware person has to induce others to accept the necessity of pattern change.

   C.   The existence and mindfulness of goals.

   D.   The accuracy of the family's perception that pattern revision is necessary.

   E.   The accuracy and thoroughness of its knowledge of future pattern requirements.

   F.   Its willingness to revise its patterns. Willingness involves:
      1.   The acceptance of short term inefficiency.
      2.   Taking risks.
      3.   The perception of long term benefit to

---

[9]   Watzlawick, et al., op. cit.

34

compensate for short term loss.

G. The evenness with which family members are affected by the inappropriateness.

H. The generalizability of its correction patterns.

I. The past effectiveness of its correction patterns.

3. The availability of time, energy, and material resources.

4. The existence of outside assistance and the family's ability and willingness to use it.

5. Its stage in the life cycle.

6. Constancy in its social context.

7. The family's good fortune.

We now move to the consideration of next stage of family crisis, the stressor event.

CHAPTER 3

THE STRESSOR

In this chapter concerning the stressor, the focus moves away from family processes and turns to events that bring about changes in those processes. As we move through this part of our inquiry, we will first define the stressor and establish its place in the crisis model. In passing, we will briefly consider the stressor as emphasized in the theoretical formulations of Hill and Farber. Our next effort will be to differentiate the Stressor from the family's response to it. The remainder of the chapter will deal with a classification of stressors and I will indicate the various dimensions of stressors and explain how these dimensions differentially affect family life. Although the emphasis in this chapter is on non-family events, one important family characteristic, its ability to foresee the stressor's approach, will be considered.

THE STRESSOR DEFINED

The stressor is an important element in the crisis process. A stressor is a particular circumstance or situation which forces at least one family member to be aware that inappropriateness exists in the family's current patterns. The stressor can be related to the inappropriateness of either correction or execution patterns; it can be associated with a community-wide situation or with a private one. In any case, the stressor marks a point at which there is the awareness on the part of at least one family member that family life must change from what it was.

In the crisis model, the Stressor marks the end of the Period of Incipience. It ushers in the Secondary Adjustment Period, that period in which the family either struggles to reorganize and rid itself of inappropriateness or opts for non-reorganization and heads toward transformation.

In considering Incipience and Stressors, it is helpful to consider the work of Farber and Hill. The Period of Incipience has no counterpart in the theories of either man. Farber wrote[1] of an "initial organization" which is distorted and this distortion is the crisis for it requires the family to develop new processes. Hill wrote that the

---

[1]   Farber, op. cit., pp. 392-394.

family has a repertory of crisis-meeting resources[2] and these resources are employed by the family after the crisis-provoking event takes place. Hill's conceptualization is not highly developed in the area of the family's resources and recovery. Hill classified stressors because, apparently, he believed that the different kinds of stressors had different effects on families. Farber did not classify the stressors, as he was more concerned with the family's creative response.

This model takes a middle road. With Farber, I am more interested in family interaction than with the classification of the stressors, and yet, I agree with Hill that stressors affect families in different ways. It is to this differential effect that we now turn our attention. Our first step in understanding the stressor's effect is to separate its impact from the family's reaction to it. This separation will isolate the subject under discussion, the stressor's impact, and hopefully, clarity will thereby be advanced.

SEPARATING STRESSOR FROM RESPONSE

As McCubbin indicated[3], conceptualization and related research are improved by distinguishing between "the stressors...and the dependent variables of family responses and adjustments". We will soon see that making this distinction is not easy and yet its importance requires that we attempt to differentiate stressor from response. I will suggest a line of thought which you may find helpful.

Separating stressor from response is difficult because a stressor's effect is in part determined by the family's response to it. That which is a stressor for one family is "business as usual" for some other group. The family member's definition of an event as a stressor and the way the other members process that definition are highly idiosyncratic and are crucial to determining the extent to which the event is stressful.

This however, is only part of the story. Certain events have a much greater potential to disturb families than do other events. For example, the death of a family member has a greater impact than a child's failure in school; financial ruin has a greater impact than a move to a different house; retirement is likely to have more of an impact than a breadwinner's short illness. And so forth. I'm saying that, independent of the family response, certain stressors

---

[2] Hill, "Generic Features of Families Under Stress," op. cit., p. 143.
[3] McCubbin et al., op. cit., p. 857.

38

disturb the family's internal processes more than do others and, moreover, the differential effect can be attributed to certain of the stressor's characteristics.

Isolating the stressor is achieved by considering it to be external to the family system. If the family system is defined as including the current family members and their existing relationships, the idea of the stressor's external nature can be more easily grasped. The stressor is external because it is not a part (it is neither a member nor a relationship) but an event which affects a part or the whole. Not being a part of the system, it is external to it.

Said another way, at a given time, a particular family system is set: its membership is fixed and its patterns are established. No stressor is present in the system. Then, a stressor occurs and the system is upset as either the personnel changes or the relationships change or both changes occur. That which upsets the system comes from outside it because the stressor is neither the members nor their relationships but that which changed these components.

This being external is easy to see when the stressor is transactional as when the breadwinner loses his job. The external nature is much less easy to see if the stressor is interactional or developmental or both as when an adolescent leaves home. I believe that even an event such as this is best seen as external because it happens to an established system. Even though the agent who brings the stressor to the system has family membership, the stressor is still external. Any event that is not at the level of the family system, whether it be at a more general level (societal) or more specific level (personal) is external to the system. In the example of the adolescent's leaving home, the event is a change that occurs first in the adolescent's life and this is initially at the personal level. The adolescent later brings the stressor to the family and the family responds.[4]

You will recall that the purpose of this discussion has been to separate the stressor event from the family's reaction so that the classification of stressors could occur without being confounded by family characteristics. It is to that classification that we now turn.

CLASSIFICATION OF STRESSORS

In this section, I will classify stressors on the basis

---

[4] "An Aside On Conceptualization" is included at the end of the chapter in which I explain why I believe that considering the stressor's source does not help in understanding its impact.

of certain of their characteristics, these characteristics tend to make a difference in the stressor's power to affect the family. As indicated above, the family's response to the stressor is likely to be the major contributing factor to the disorganization which the stressor brings to the family and yet the stressor's qualities have an effect which should not be overlooked.

The classification will begin with a discussion of normative and non-normative stressors and then the family's ability to foresee will be considered. Since normative aspects and the family's ability to foresee are the two most influential factors in determining the stressor's impact, or so I believe, these two elements will be then considered together. Following that, we will explore other characteristics of stressors which, although important, seem to me to be of lesser importance in influencing the degree of impact.

Stressors: Major Elements

The effect that a stressor has on the family is primarily a function of two factors. The first factor is the nature of the stressor: whether or not it could be anticipated. Some stressors are clearly predictable (a birth, a retirement) and other stressors cannot be anticipated (an accidental death). Whether or not a stressor is predictable is a property of the stressor and has to do with whether most families experience the stressor sometime in their journey through time or whether the event is rare and most families avoid it. The former is a "normative" stressor; the latter is called "non-normative."

The other factor related to the stressor's effect is the family's ability to foresee what lies in store for them. Since some families perceive the trouble ahead and successfully avoid it while other families do not, a property of the family is indicated. This property is the family's ability to foresee and to act appropriately.

In this chapter, we will focus on the stressor's effect as this is related to stressor predictability and the family's ability to foresee. Family foresight will be considered after the discussion of the stressor's normativeness. First, however, there are terminological confusions that should be straightened out.

In referring to an unpublished manuscript by Hill and Joy, McCubbin writes of normative cries as those "which occur in most families and serve as demarcation points for stages in the family life cycle".[5] Following the

---

[5] McCubbin, op. cit., p. 860.

40

developmental perspective, the demarcation points are related to the role changes which reflect the growth and development of children and the concomitant changes in family life and organization.

For the purposes of this model, we will not limit "normative" to child-associated changes but emphasize two other ideas: First, that normative stressors are ubiquitous in that they occur to most families and that they are expectable in that a family can expect them to occur at certain points.[6] While most have to do with children, there are other normative stressors such as retirement and death with which all family units must contend.

Lipman-Blumen refers to the idea of "normative" as "expectability" and remarks that the important element is the "degree to which the crisis could be expected or predicted."[7] She contrasts "expectability" with "randomness", the latter referring to what we have termed non-normative. Non-normative stressors are those which "come out of the blue" and affect only some families. They are unexpected, can not be predicted, and families have little or no chance to prepare for them.

Stressors: predictable or unpredictable. If the stressor is normative and could have been anticipated, the resulting family dynamics are quite different than if the stressor was unpredictable. An example of a normative stressor is the birth of the first child; a non-normative stressor is exemplified by the birth of a severely mentally retarded child. The family dynamics that result are different because a normative and therefore predictable stressor allows time for the family to correct its patterns and the process of correction can be well thought out and generally agreed upon. This is not to say that rational problem solving always accompanies normative stressors, it says only that rational problem solving could occur. With this type of stressor, correction can take place during Incipience when the family is not under pressure for immediate pattern revision.

Non-normative and therefore unpredictable stressors affect families whose patterns, both execution and correction, are appropriate. This kind of stressor can happen to any family and the family's strength or weakness is relevant only after the stressor has taken place.

Unpredictable stressors require that family patterns be changed after the stressor and not before. Pattern revision following a stressor is frequently more rushed, the

---

[6]   Ibid.
[7]   Lipman-Blumen, op. cit., p. 890.

opportunity for consensus is lessened, and authoritarian processes are more likely. In addition, other problems arise because the stressor's abruptness makes it more difficult for the family to adequately function in other areas. Lastly, it is likely that a long term solution will not be forthcoming for the family's first priority will be the alleviation of current intense difficulties. Clearly, the impact of the stressor is greater if the family has had no opportunity to prepare itself for its coming. This differential in impact can be directly traced to the stressor's characteristics.

Stressors: whether foreseen or not. The other factor which has a major bearing on the stressor's impact is whether or not the family sees its approach. The family's ability to foresee the stressor's coming is different from the normative or non-normative nature of the stressor for to foresee or not is in the family domain and the relative normativeness is a property of the stressor. The reader would do well to remember that this discussion regarding foresight, in as much as it pertains to family characteristics, is the one exception to the rule that this chapter would deal with non-family influences.

To foresee in this sense means two things: (1) the understanding that the family is headed for a stressor and (2) the correcting of the situation so the stressor is either avoided or its effect minimized. Only normative stressors can be foreseen. The birth of a child is such an predictable stressor. Some families foresee the birth as problematic and reorganize their lives accordingly. Other families do not foresee the problems and the necessary reorganization must take place after the blessed event.

Implications of this classification. This classification of stressors provides a unique way for looking at families and raises important questions. At this time we can only raise the questions; research is necessary to find definitive answers. Some of these questions refer to the stressor's predictability. If a stressor is predictable, does this improve the family's chances to successfully deal with it? Is there more difficulty in adjusting after the stressor than before? Do unpredictable stressors create more problems for families than predictable ones?

There are other questions and these concern the family's ability to foresee stressors and the particular nature of stressors. In Figure IV, these considerations are presented. Families in Cell 1 foresee the predictable stressors and, by making the necessary corrections, avoid the stressor's most deleterious effects. Inquiry into these families would center on how they do this. Investigation would answer such questions as; Who saw the problem first? How did the aware person get the others to share their definition? How did action result? Was their

FIGURE IV

TYPES OF STRESSORS (PREDICTABLE OR NOT)
BY FAMILY'S ABILITY TO FORESEE

		Stressor's Nature			
		Predict- able		Unpredict- able	
FAMILY'S	Foresee	1		2	
STENGTH	Not Foresee	3A	3B	4A	4B

correction unrushed, marked by consensus, and based on sweet reason? What are the characteristics of such families? What are their communication patterns? How does the presence of children affect their success? What are their problem solving techniques? Their level of marriage satisfaction? and on and on.

Cell 2 is a blank cell, for no family can foresee something which is not predictable. The only way that families can deal with unpredictable stressors before their occurrence is to insure against them. In the sense of life insurance, or auto insurance, this preparation is financial and affects interaction patterns only in a secondary way.

Those in Cell 3 have not foreseen what they might have. As a result, they experience the stressor and subsequent activity. Some families are successful in meeting the challenges of the stressor, those in the 3A part of the cell, and some are unsuccessful, those in the 3B section. The following questions are salient. Were the family members ignorant of what was coming? If so, why did they not know? If they saw what was coming, why did they not act to remedy the situation? Were their correction patterns inadequate? Were they unable to arrive at consensus? Did they have too much invested in their inappropriate patterns to make a change? Were their personal inadequacies carried over from their families of orientation? Did society mystify the situation in such a way that correct appraisal of the situation was impossible?

Then, too, what were the differences between the families that were successful (3A) and those who were not (3B)? Neither of these classifications contain families who foresaw that they might have and yet there appear to be differences in characteristics which enable one group to master a situation while the other succumbs to it. What are these characteristics? What are the adjustments that are necessary after the stressor? How do the families in Cell 3A differ from those in Cell 1? and so forth.

In Cell 4 are those families who experience an unpredictable stressor. Some of these families successfully cope with the stressors, those classified as 4A; others are unsuccessful, the 4B families, and never recover from the damaging experience. Further research would serve to isolate, classify, and explore the characteristics of the families in each category.

The idea emerges that effectively functioning families revise their patterns and avoid stressors and that ineffective families fail to make the necessary correction until a stressor forces them to do so. My intention in the preceding discussion was to indicate the importance of and interplay between the stressor's property of predictability and the family's ability to foresee, this importance being relevant to the stressor's impact on the family. Normative stressors allow families with foresight to make correction and avoid the worst effects; non-normative stressors make no such allowance and fall upon families, both able and unable. With non-normative stressors, families respond after the event, effective families responding successfully and ineffective ones failing. These responses to the stressor are considered in more depth in the next chapter but, before getting involved in those considerations, there are some other elements of the stressor which influence its effect and it is to these that we now turn.

Other Characteristics of the Stressor

The effect of the stressor is in part a function of its characteristics and the most important characteristic, predictability, has been discussed. But other elements of the stressor affect its ability to upset a family and these elements can be conceptualized as a series of continuua. These continuua follow:

Source: Interactional or transactional[*]

Effect: Whole family or one part

Onset: Gradual or abrupt

---

[*] See "An Aside On Conceptualization" at this chapter's end for consideration of this dimension.

Extent: Transitory or chronic[9]

Each dimension, except "source", will be considered from the standpoint of its impact, the intensity of its effect.

Effect: whole family or one part. A stressor's effect partially depends upon who in the family is affected by it. The stressor's effect is a function of the number of family members who feel the impact and the particular family members who feel the impact most strongly. A stressor's impact will be greatest if all members are affected and least if only one or a small number of less powerful individuals are affected.

A few examples might help. The destruction of a home by fire or flood will be stressful because all family members are affected in that all lose some of their possessions and "space" and each has to rearrange their daily lives. An adolescent's leaving home is less of a stressor for younger brothers and sisters and, in all liklihood, the adolescent's father will feel only a marginal effect. This particular stressor may be felt by the mother most strongly especially if she has remained at home and invested her life in the child but, for the others, it is business as usual and the stressor's overall effect will be minimal.

The system's perspective leads to the conclusion that a stressor's effect will be limited for only a brief period of time, the effect will soon become greater or lesser. If the person or persons most severely affected are powerful family members, the problem will spread itself around as other elements of the family's functioning are affected. If those most affected are marginal to family functioning, these being children, peripheral husband/father types, or

---

[9] This list is derived from Jean Lipman-Blumen's "A Typology of Crisis." She conceptualized ten dimensions which include the four just listed and Randomness-Expectability which has been previously discussed. The other five she listed were not used because two of them, Natural versus Man-made generation and Scarcity versus Surplus, do not seem to me to be very important; one, Intensity versus Mildness, is what we are attempting to explore and is therefore of a higher level; one other one, Perceived solvability versus Perceived insolvability, refers to the family's characteristics. The last of her ten has to do with substantive content, "it subsumes a set of subject areas" and is a different kind of classification. Of the four listed above, I have retained the name of just one, "Transitoriness versus Chronicity", the other names being changed to more commonly used words or words with a special meaning in the model. Lipman-Blumen, op. cit., p. 890.

inconsequential wife/mothers, the stressor's impact will decrease because other family members will not be affected and the impacted one will have to deal with what must be then seen as a personal problem. The stressor's impact will become intensified if the powerful and important are affected; its impact will be less if marginally `powerful family functionaries are affected.

Onset: gradual or abrupt. If a stressor comes to the family gradually it will have less impact than one which comes from "out of the blue" with no warning whatsoever. The same stressor event, say the death of a family member, will have a substantially different effect if it is accidental and therefore abrupt than if the death follows a long illness, diagnosed early as terminal. With abruptness comes the immediate need for pattern change, no chance for the revision of thinking, and no opportunity for practising with alternatives.

Extent: transitory or chronic. Transitory stressors are those that occur only once; chronic stressors recur, repeating themselves over and over. Transitory stressors represent short-term problems and chronic stressors are associated with long-standing difficulties. The alcoholism of a family member is frequently associated with stressor events which recur; the birth of a first child occurs but once.

The effect of each of these stressor types is different, not necessarily more or less, only different. A transitory stressor happens once and is passed, the family is left with an accomplished event and must then pick up the pieces of its shattered life. There may well be a sense of finality, a movement to a new life stage or new situation. Transitory stressors call for new arrangements, new ways, and new approaches; a successful family's efforts will be aimed at developing new patterns so as to establish a workable and revised family system.

Chronic stressors affect families because they recur and repeatably upset families. They are a drain on family resources. Their impact is extensive and different from the transitory stressors which have a more intensive effect. Their recurring nature gives families a chance to "practise" dealing with them and families frequently adapt. Some do so by dealing effectively with the recurring stressor by adapting other patterns so as to accomodate the recurring event. Other families become numb and isolate the problem by seeking compensating satisfaction elsewhere, either in the system or outside. There is no clean break with the past as with transitory stressors; in fact, the past is, in many ways, the present.

The stressor brings to an end a family's being able to live with a particular pattern, now inappropriate, in its

46

habitual way. The stressor forces onto the consciousness of at least one family member that some pattern needs revision. By so doing, it interjects into the family a new definition of the family's situation and ushers in the Period of Secondary Adjustment. In these cases, the stressor ends the Period of Incipience and the family enters a new phase of experience and, in this phase, either moves to resolve its difficulties or heads toward transformation.

Since this chapter has concentrated on stressors and I have made a point of separating these from the family's reactions, the summary section on family strengths will be omitted.

AN ASIDE ON CONCEPTUALIZATION

The source of the stressor has been historically considered (in Hill's 1958 pioneer classification)[10] and is currently seen (in Lipman-Blumen's 1975 classification)[11] as being a factor which affects the stresor's impact. From my discussion early in the chapter on the separation of the stressor from the family's response and from the omission of "source" from the list of salient stressor characteristics, it is obvious that I step outside this theoretical tradition. I will briefly explain the reasons why I disagree with the idea that the stressor's source, its externality or internality, is important to an understanding of its impact.

First, I believe that the source of the stressor has been mistakenly considered to be important because, in the earliest formulation, Hill confused the stressor with the family's response. He stated, "If the blame for the stressor can be placed outside the family, the stress may solidify rather than disorganize the family."[12] Later, he accented the same point by saying that interactional stressors "reflect poorly on the family's internal adequacy." It seems clear to me that Hill confused the family's definition ("blame being placed" and "reflect poorly") with the stressor's characteristics.[13]

---

[10] Hill, "Generic Features of Families Under Stress," op. cit.

[11] Lipman-Blumen, op. cit., p. 890.

[12] Hill, "Generic Features of Families Under Stress," op. cit., p. 142.

[13] Ibid. This analysis, of course, can not (nor could it) take anything away from the important work by Hill in the development of crisis theory. The progress that has been made, (which is evident in the more recent work of Hill and also that of Burr and Lipman-Blumen, McCubbin and others) has been based on this early pioneer effort.

47

Secondly, I believe that theoretical formulations since Hill have just made the assumption that source is important and dealt with the issue at face value. I believe there are insufficient logical reasons to warrant treating source as an important variable and, of course, research is as yet unavailable. I believe that the family's definition of the source is important, in fact, in the next Chapter I indicate my belief that the family's positing of source is crucial. To say that the family's definition of source is vital is quite different from saying that the "real" source is important.

There is a third reason. This reason has to do with the inability to tell what is the "real" source of the stressor. This inability arises because the family receives many influences from outside and responds to them and the influences and responses feed upon each other until they are so mixed that the result is of the "chicken and egg and which came first?" variety. An alcohol problem of a family member, the related vocational difficulty, and the associated perverse family interaction is an example in which all three system levels, personal, familial, and social, are temporally inter-related such that the determination of cause and effect is impossible.

Not only is there a cause and effect problem from the standpoint of time, there is confusion resulting from mixed dynamics. It is simply impossible to sort out what "causes" what. For example, Vogel and Bell state that a child's emotional disturbance and attendant school failure (an external matter) is associated with a particular kind of parenting behavior (an internal matter). Moreover, they indicate that this parenting style is a reflection of a particular spousal style (another internal matter) but that the spousal style reflects a personal inability to deal with tensions associated with a job related (or other external) matter.[14] In this example, the family's dynamics are mixed with both social and personal dynamics and waves of cause and effect move back and forth from one dimension to another. External problems (school and job difficulties) grow concomitantly with internal inadequacies (personal, spousal, family incompetence).

So, for these reasons, I believe that the stressor's source, when considered in isolation to the family's definition, is not important in determining its impact.

But, what about the source that is clearly external? What about, say, a flood or tornado, or war separation? I would agree that these are external and as Hill said, may help solidify the family. They may, also, disorganize the

---

[14] Vogel and Bell, op. cit.

family; the difference in effect still seems to be the family's definition. As for those stressors which appear to be internal, I am at a loss to think of any that could not be defined as having their source outside. So, what I see is an inability to separate internal difficulties from outside influences and, even in situations in which the stressor is more clearly external, one of the other stressor dimensions (effect, onset, or extent) can be more advantageously used because of its greater clarity in differentiating the family's response from the stressor's properties.

There is one other small matter, that concerning the stressor's variable impact as this impact is affected by its voluntary or involuntary nature. Adams[15] indicated this to be one of the two most important dimensions of the stressor. Since I have not used it, I will briefly explain why.

Volition, freedom of will, the voluntariness of behavior are rather outside the scope of this model. I earlier indicated my belief that there could be freedom of action, that people and groups of people could do more than only respond, that they could also act. I continue to hold those ideas to be true but I also believe that much behavior is reactive and that you and I and our associated groups frequently are forced (for example, by limited or non-existent alternatives) to act in particular ways. To say that behavior can be volitional is not the same thing as saying that it always is. And, so, a question arises about whether an act is voluntary or not.

Whether an act is voluntary or not is never really knowable. "Voluntariness" and "involuntariness" are characteristics that are attributed to one person by another as a means of explaining the other's behavior. Whether an act is voluntary or not can never be known for sure because of the inability to know motives, alternatives, precedents, and goals, and the manifold other elements which get involved. And besides, as soon as we begin to deal with one person's definition of another's behavior, we move into other matters, the family's definition of behavior, and move away from our major concern of this chapter, the qualities of the stressor. Elements of definition are discussed in the next chapter in which the focus is on the Secondary Adjustment Period.

---

[15] Bert Adams, The Family: A Sociological Interpretation (Chicago: Rand McNally, 1975), p. 339.

CHAPTER 4

SECONDARY ADJUSTMENT PERIOD AND REVIEW

To this point, the model has been concerned with the family's need to change and its difficulty in doing so. This need to change was created by pattern inappropriateness and this was made apparent to at least one family member by the stressor. In the Secondary Adjustment Period, the family must deal with the awareness that something is wrong. The family's success depends on the mobilization of its correction patterns. In this section, we will see how some families successfully proceed and eventually take appropriate action. We will see how other families, those with ineffective correction patterns, never deal successfully with the stressor-indicated problem. As LeMasters said:[1]

> Finally, the cases in the sample confirm what the previous studies in this area have shown: that the event itself is only one factor determining the extent and severity of the crisis on any given family. Their resources, their previous experience with crisis, the pattern of role re-organization before the crisis - these factors are equally important in determining the total reaction to the crisis.

In our consideration of the Secondary Adjustment Period, we will be concerned with the family's reaction (creative and otherwise) to the stressor.

This chapter has two major parts, the first part explores the Secondary Adjustment Period by first looking at elements which promote pattern persistence: the family's need to be both instrumental and integrated and its efforts to maintain a balance between flexibility and consistency. This is followed by an overview of the steps of Secondary Adjustment and a section concerning how speed enhances success. Each step of Secondary Adjustment is then explained. The chapter's second half introduces a different way of looking at crisis and the process which extends from Incipience through Secondary Adjustment is reviewed using this new view.

---

[1]   LeMasters, op. cit., p. 355.

THE SECONDARY ADJUSTMENT PERIOD

Persistence

On the surface, it would appear that the family's problem is a simple one. After all, an inappropriate pattern has been brought to light and needs to be fixed. The family ought to be aware of the problem and they should know that they must find the solution. Unfortunately, the situation is more complex than that.

Integration and instrumentality. A factor contributing to the complexity is the necessity of balancing integration and instrumentality, that is, keeping the family together and getting things done. "There must be discipline, rules and division of labor . . . in the family and there must be solidarity among the units comprising [the family] . . . in order for the system to function adequately."[2] A family with an instrumental orientation such that integration is sacrificed to the god Efficiency is in trouble right away. A loss of integration reduces cooperation and possibilities for harmonious interaction. This kind of interaction is vital; meeting the member's needs for affection is generally regarded as the modern family's most important function and affect is nothing but the good feelings about self and others that are generated from harmonious cooperative relationships.

Moreover, the family's response to the stressor cannot be so totally instrumental that it rejects its own ideology and history. With the rejection of the value of its former way of living, the family is emptied of content and becomes, as Kingsley Davis said in another context, an "empty caricature". This form-without-substance has no validity and no meaning; form may very likely crumble before new content can be added.

On the other hand, the family can not be totally dedicated to generating good feelings. There are tasks that need to be done: family members must be fed and clothed and housed and this requires that money be brought in and spent wisely. These are important elements of family life but most families do not stop there. Family members become educated, they develop special skills, and they are active in many ways. They enjoy each other and feel good about themselves; they grow. The coordination of all this, the basics and the "priceless unessentials"[3] is very complicated and success

---

[2] Alice Rossi, "Transition to Parenthood," *Journal of Marriage and the Family*, 30, 1968, p. 37.

[3] Hansen and Hill, *op. cit.*, pp. 787-789; Walter B. Cannon, *The Wisdom of the Body* (New York: Norton, 1932), p. 323.

entails a high level of instrumentality.

Instrumentality and integration are very closely associated and it is difficult to imagine a family continuing for a long time without both elements being liberally present. Maintaining a fulfilling personal existence with satisfying family relations within an integrated and efficient family is a challenging goal. This is especially challenging during crisis when old balances are reassuring but inoperative and new balances are necessary but not yet determined.

There is another factor with contributes to pattern persistence: that factor is related to the family's maintaining a balance between consistency and flexibility. In the next section, our focus will be on that.

Consistency and flexibility. At this point in the crisis process, the family has learned that it must make a break with the past for the stressor has indicated that things cannot be as they were. The family's viability requires that former patterns be changed. Yet, this change must take place in a situation in which interaction has predictability and the family has a consistent theme. Behavior and ideology reinforce each other and provide family members with a sense of what the family means. Flexibility is limited by the essential need for this consistency.

The achievement and maintenance of the balance between consistency and flexibility is made difficult by the family's definition of itself. We are indebted to R.D. Laing for the idea of 'family' as, not the objective collection of people, but, the idea of the family as contained in the thoughts of each family member.[4] All members of a family define the collection of individuals in a generally similar way. This definition, this 'family', contains rules of relationship, the family's meaning, and its place in time and space. To the extent that there is agreement, there is something like a group mind which is generated.

A stressor or a family member's deviation throws into question the whole matter of 'family' and the family members must sort out the way they think about each other and their group. This sorting out is difficult for 'family' notions are inextricably tied to powerful images of self and self-with-others and these images are very slow to change. The maintenance of the group mind requires the meeting of individual minds and this meeting is problematic for it is extremely unlikely that individual minds will be identically

---

[4] R.D. Laing, The Politics of the Family and Other Essays (New York: Vintage, 1972), pp. 3-19.

affected by a problem and equally able to adapt to its solution. As a result, the family's redefinition of itself takes time.

So, the family must change (the stressor has indicated that) but change must be managed so that the family members maintain shared images of themselves, of each other, and of the family unit. It takes time for this shared image to be established for there is the tendency to refer back to pre-stressor patterns which were comfortable, albeit inappropriate. Therefore, 'family' is associated with inertia; it serves to make the family less flexible.

We now turn our attention to a consideration of the steps involved in the Secondary Adjustment Period; these steps occur as the family creatively responds to or non-creatively reels under the stressor's impact. Each of these steps will be later considered more thoroughly.

The Process of Secondary Adjustment: An Overview

In the Secondary Adjustment Period, the family's ability to successfully balance consistency and flexibility, integration and instrumentality, is tested in each of five sequential steps. These steps are shown in Figure V and an overview of them will be presently undertaken. Since progress through the steps is not automatic, because some families have to start over or retrace their actions, Exits and Repeat Loops will also be explained. This section will end with an example drawn from a real-life situation.

An overview of the steps. At the start, at least one family member must be aware of pattern inappropriateness and the necessity of revision. If the aware member can convince others of the problem's existence, the family has attained the second step. Once they agree that there is a problem, they must reach consensus as to the solution.[5] To this point, the problem has been one of definition and now a different type of behavior is necessary: action, taking action is the fourth step. Finally, for successful families, suitable action is taken and inappropriate patterns are corrected. With suitable action the Secondary Adjustment Period is completed and the family takes one of the routes

----

[5]   Consensus is a word usually associated with the give and take process of negotiation and the resulting agreement. As here used, "consensus" indicates agreement and does not denote characteristics of the agreement-reaching process. The agreement may be negotiated, it may be the result of naked power, or it may be the product of guile and more covert operations. The method of reaching consensus is not as important to short term family viability as is the consensus itself.

to Reorganization, the final stage of the crisis process.

Success during Secondary Adjustment is indicated by the family's movement through the five step sequence. That is, a family emerges successfully when their inappropriate patterns are corrected as this inappropriateness was indicated by the stressor.

Exits and Repeat Loops. The family that successfully moves through this period from Stressor to Restructuring is shown to move through awareness, decision making, and action. This progression is problematic and success is not guaranteed. Both the stressor and the family's internal dynamics may be such that the awareness of inappropriateness will not be shared by others. In this case, the family takes Exit 1. Likewise, the collective sharing of the definition of the problem does not guarantee consensus as to solution. If no agreement can be reached about a solution, Exit 2 is taken. Moreover, a family may be able to reach consensus as to the right solution but be unable to take the necessary corrective steps. They take Exit 3. Finally, they may never arrive at a suitable action despite repeated attempts and so they take Exit 4. Failure to move to any one of these steps (that is, the taking of any exit) will move the family toward either continued inappropriateness or separation and transformation. In a move toward continued inappropriateness, the family stays together but replays the same scenario, that is, it repeats the same inappropriate patterns that existed prior to the stressor. Another stressor will again bring about a new Secondary Adjustment Period.

Another possibility exists. Adequately functioning families that have reached the action stage may find that their action is unsuitable, that is, that their action does not solve their problem. Since their correction patterns are working well they do not revert to pattern inappropriateness and another stressor. However, they do need to repeat the steps after the shared definition of pattern inadequacy. By using the Repeat Loop, they go half way back and attempt to more accurately define the problem or select a better solution or attempt other action. By taking the Repeat Loop, a family can attempt another decision-action sequence and move into this sequence at the point where they perceive previous sequences to have been inefficacious.

In Figure V, it can be seen that a family can enter the Secondary Adjustment Period several times by taking an exit, repeating the inappropriate pattern, and experiencing the same type of stressor. Each time the sequence is repeated the likelihood of ultimate success is lessened. As Hill said, "Successful experience with crisis tests and strengthens a family but defeat in crisis is punitive of

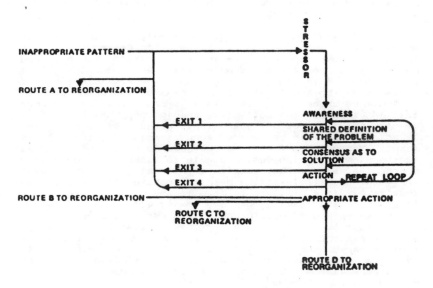

Figure V SECONDARY ADJUSTMENT PERIOD

family structure and morale."[*] Defeat, that is, the continued inappropriateness of the pattern, is made evident by the repetition of the stressor.

Each time the stressor comes around, it points to family inadequacy and this inadequacy must be handled in addition to the inappropriate pattern. Seen another way, to the failure to correct an inappropriate execution pattern is added the problem of an inadequate correction pattern. For example, let's say that a wife cannot get her husband to share her perception that a financial problem exists. When, at the end of another month, there again is insufficient money, the couple must deal with the insufficiency and the fact that nothing was done previously. Because of prior ineffectiveness, one of them may feel a sense of failure and this feeling is a complicating factor. One of them has invested in the status quo, in the maintenance of an inappropriate pattern. The next time around, this investment must be handled as well as the problem of the inappropriate pattern.

An example, I offer the following to illustrate the use of exits and repeated inappropriateness and stressors. The example might also dispel the idea that a stressor must be a major event, both powerful and dramatic.

A young woman in her early thirties who knew of this model, we'll call her Brenda, talked to me about her recent marital separation and the following is a recreation of that conversation. She asked me to help her apply the model to her experience.

J.   Well, according to the model, there has to be something which brings to the awareness of at least one family member that patterns will have to be corrected. This doesn't square with your experience?

B.   I can't think of one big event. Sure, there were lots of smaller events which happened over the years but no one real stressor.

J.   These events that happened over the years. Did they have some common theme?

B.   Yes. They all were the result of my getting angry with my husband because he left me to run the house and raise the children and was very distant from all of us and the whole family scene.

---

[*]   Hill, "Generic Features of Families Under Stress," op. cit., p. 148.

J. How were these resolved?

B. They never really were. He would listen to me for a while and then turn me off, I mean you could see him begin to mentally wander off and his responses became vague. I would get tired of this and he would go off to the office.

J. How frequently did this occur?

B. About two or three times a year.

J. But now you have separated. What immediately preceded this decision.

B. We went out to dinner on a Friday evening with some clients of his and I must have got some bad food for the next morning I woke up physically sick with the throwing-up and the whole scene. My husband left the house in the morning and went to his office even though I was in no condition to look after things at home. He said he'd be home in the early afternoon but when my daughter tried to call him his secretary said he had gone to see a customer. He came home in the early evening and said he was exhausted and went to bed for the night. On Sunday I was feeling some better but I was still terribly weak but he left for a one-day workshop, which he hadn't even planned on attending, on a specialized part of his work. Even though the workshop was over after dinner, he didn't come until eleven o'clock.

J. What happened when he returned?

B. I was furious. I pointed out that this indicated a lack of concern for me and showed the great distance that existed between us. Also, that I was not willing to stand for it any longer and that we would have to get professional help if we were to stay together.

J. Did he agree to seeing a marriage counselor?

B. Yes.

J. We'll come back in a moment to what happened in therapy, but first, tell me how the situation that you just mentioned differed from those other angry times that occurred in the past.

B. It really wasn't all that different. That is why I'm asking if the stressor has to be an explosion. It just seemed to me that this was the last straw and that I could no longer live with him if he was not going to share more.

J.   What happened in therapy?

B.   The counselor asked each of us how we could change
     the relationship to make it more satisfying. My
     husband said that it was perfectly fine with him
     the way it was and that any change that would
     require more family involvement would be
     unacceptable to him.

J.   And you?

B.   I told him that I wanted a relationship where the
     other person cared about me and showed it by being
     around and participating in the family.

J.   What happened?

B.   My husband said that this was not him and that a
     divorce was the only solution.

J.   One more question and then we'll get to the model.
     You mentioned before that this event wasn't
     substantially different from others that had
     preceded it over the years. Can you think of
     anything that would set it apart?

B.   No, like I said. I just got good and fed up.

J.   You must have been fed up before.

B.   Yes, but this time I could see this unsatisfactory
     relationship continuing on indefinitely and that
     without help there was no way that I could get the
     ... have the kind of relationship that I wanted?

J.   Hm. What were you fed up with?

B.   I've told you. His being so remote.

J.   Yes, but you have been distant from each other for
     years.

B.   If there is something else it would have to be the
     idea that my husband was so distant that this
     distance itself made it impossible for us to ever
     correct the situation.

J.   OK. From the standpoint of the model, here is how
     I would look at what you have told me. First, a
     pattern was established early in your marriage
     that your husband was not to be heavily involved
     on the home front. I don't know what the pay-offs
     were for you, of course, but you were willing to

59

put up with it for one reason or another.

B. Well, he started making good money right away and I was busy with the children and all that.

J. You did not totally accept the situation, however, for you became angry and let him have it about his lack of interest. These minor blow-ups can be seen as stressor-related for you were aware that something needed to be changed. Your awareness was never accepted, the two of you never reached consensus, and you and your husband returned to Incipience and continued the same patterns. So far so good?

B. Yes.

J. I would suspect that there was a general escalating quality to these periodical reactions. Did they get progressively more violent?

B. The first ones were not much more than sharp exchanges. After awhile they became arguments and eventually out-and-out fights. ·Not physical, of course.

J. From the standpoint of the model, that fits. Each time you went through one of these incidents you not only had the incident to deal with but you also had the resentment that you had to deal with the same kind of incident for a second time or third time. This generated more anger and hopelessness. I suspect that it was this that finally brought about the break. The hopelessness of being in a situation which could not be corrected and the unwillingness on your part to continue to do so led to a change in the kind of solution. Before, the two of you had reached some kind of satisfactory relationship involving a lot of separateness. You became unwilling to live with this and would no longer be put-off. The use of a therapist was an attempt to restructure the system in a way more agreeable to you. Your husband, in terms of his desire for distance, surprisingly agreed and then used the therapeutic session to increase the distance between the two of you to the point of separation. You agreed and the appropriate action was finally taken.

This completes the overview of the Secondary Adjustment Period. In this overview we have traced the family's movements after the stressor and had theory made manifest in a real-life situation involving repeated inappropriateness and eventual appropriate action in family transformation. We now move to the next section which explains why success is

60

advanced by a family's swift movement through Secondary Adjustment and this will be followed by an in-depth consideration of each of the steps of secondary adjustment.

The Need for Speed

Success during the Secondary Adjustment Period is promoted if the family quickly moves through this crisis stage. The more time a family takes in finding a solution and acting on it, the less likely will be their success. The Secondary Adjustment Period is a time of disorganization and this disorganization fosters other difficulties. When families are working to solve difficult problems, much of their energy is devoted to survival. The result is that there is no energy left for the priceless unessentials, the reasons (intimacy, need fulfillment, companionship, etc.) for which they got together in the first place. The family in the Secondary Adjustment Period is likely to be a drag as it has directed its energies toward surviving and there is no time for fun. The family can lose sight of its original purpose and the less time its purpose is lost, the better are the family's chances for success.

As an aside, there exist other families whose purpose is not to provide priceless unessentials; their purpose is to promote family members' success in other institutions. Speed is important for those families also. For example, families of politicians are frequently organized around the transactional requirements of the heavily involved person. The family meaning is derived from publically recognized success. Since these families are oriented toward outside accomplishment, their emphasis on the priceless unessentials can well be a crisis. Yet, these families reflect the importance of moving quickly through crisis for the less time they must spend on generating good feelings, the sooner they can return to advancing their goals and the less will be the disorganization and negative affect.

There is also the problem of morale. Implied throughout the model is the idea that family members share the goal that the family's existence is important. In the Secondary Adjustment Period, the task is to find ways to survive as a unit. But what if morale is low? What if a family member thinks "I just don't care?" An extended time spent in crisis hurts morale because after repeated exits, continued inappropriateness, and a series of stressors, "who cares" kind of thinking is likely. Without a desire to correct the situation, joint family effort is impossible and so, successful movement through the Secondary Adjustment Period is not possible. Delay has played a part.

And, lest delay hurt our chances for success in understanding the model, we must move to the next section. In the following description of each of the steps of the Secondary Adjustment Period, I will consider the family resources which support successful progress and the factors which make this progress difficult.

Steps Through Secondary Adjustment

During the Secondary Adjustment Period, the awareness of at least one family member must be turned into appropriate group activity. A stressor sometimes makes only one person aware; rarely do all family members grasp the gravity of the problem simultaneously. However, one person cannot solve the problem. Family problems are exactly that: family problems. The whole family[7] has had a hand in the creation of the problem and the whole family must work together if the problem is to be solved. The Secondary Adjustment Period is the time when individual perception is transformed into family action.

Awareness. The stressor makes at least one family member aware that a pattern is inappropriate. The stressor's nature serves to determine whether awareness comes to one person or to many. Some stressors intrude into the consciousness of all members nearly simultaneously. Other stressors are more likely to be known by one family member and they will be that person's sole property for a longer period of time. The family member's awareness is related to the stressor's relevance to them; personal relevance increases sensitivity. The stressor of money shortage is felt first by the family financier, her responsibility increasing her sentience. Since stressors eventually affect all members, swift sharing usually increases success chances.

Awareness of a pattern's inappropriateness is encouraged if the difficulty has a constant effect and is forceful. Alcoholism is a particularly difficult family problem because, at least in its early stages, its behavioral manifestations are erratic. Sometimes the alcoholic can function well, and other times he/she cannot. This inconstancy confuses family members and makes precise definition of the problem very difficult.

The power of the stressor also affects awareness. Even such a powerful event as the death of a family member is ritualized and given impact. The ritualization brings

---

[7] Some family members, especially those who are very young, may be a part of the problem, but are unable to be of much help in the solution. Small children have not the maturity or capability or responsibility to work with other family members to correct inappropriateness. "Whole family" means primarily the responsible adults. The arrival at consensus about both the problem and solution is an adult affair.

closure to the existence of the deceased. Fantasy ends and the survivors are strongly reminded that their lives must be restructured without the one who has been "long loved and lost awhile". [*]

Awareness is usually followed by an attempt to get others to share the definition, but this is not always the case. A family member's secrecy is promoted by a feeling that others never listen or agree, the fear of physical and/or psychological attack, and a personal investment in (and advantage from) the status quo. Personal loss in these situations exceeds the gain from disclosure.

At times, a family member will maintain silence and change themselves rather than call the attention of other family members to the problem. This usually does not solve the difficulty for personal behavior is rarely isolated. In some instances, such as the substitution of placating behavior for appropriate opposition, one person's change may delay correction and thereby exacerbate the difficulty. In other instances, however, such as the change from inebriety to sobriety, one person's change may substantially and advantageously affect family dynamics.

These factors affect the willingness of family members to share their awareness that inappropriateness exists. Without this sharing, the family takes Exit 1 and moves towards separation or continued inappropriateness. If it repeats the inappropriate pattern, another stressor will occur and activate secondary adjustment processes. This cycle (pattern inappropriateness, stressor, non-sharing, pattern inappropriateness, etc.) can be repeated many times until the discomfort becomes unbearable and either sharing takes place, or the family heads directly toward separation.

Consensus concerning the problem. In the foregoing, I have stressed how awareness is related to the effect of the stressor and the qualities of the aware person. The sharing of awareness is our next concern and this sharing depends on the family's interaction patterns and the nature of the problem. First, I will consider how interaction patterns delimit sharing and then I will explore the ways that the stressor's characteristics make sharing difficult.

Interaction patterns, especially the level of acceptance of the aware family member, are very important. Others may discount the value of the perception because

---

[*] A different analysis is that death is ritualized because it is too powerful to comprehend, not because it needs greater impact. Death is so powerful that it numbs the survivors and the ritualization redefines the event, gives it meaning, and thereby makes closure possible.

discounting this particular person is an established family pattern. Or, other family members may be less adversely affected by the problem and are thereby less able to understand the proferred definition. It may be that others find the present situation advantagous and they are therefore unwilling to change. They reject the new definition as their first defense against change.

A shared definition is promoted by certain family characteristics. The family members must be able to communicate effectively. Good communication skills have been stressed lately and "keeping the lines of communication open" has achieved cliche status. Communication (clear and unambiguous statements about feelings and ideas made to others who are willing to invest the time and energy necessary to create harmony of meaning) is vital, it is necessary but not sufficient. That is, the sharing of a problem requires good communication skills, but these are not enough in themselves.

Communication skills require a particular kind of family setting if they are to be employed effectively. The particular climate is one which Gibb calls "supportive". This is different from the defensive climate and is marked by emotional closeness not distance, by description rather than evaluation, by an emphasis on problem solving instead of behavior control, by spontaneity not manipulation, by equality not status differences, and by provisionalism rather than dogmatism. The more supportive the climate, the less distortion for, as "defenses are reduced, the receivers become better able to concentrate upon the structure, the content, and the cognitive meanings of the message".[9]

Reaching consensus about the problem is enhanced by shared goals. If a family member believes her goals are inconsistent with those of others in her family, if she believes that her personal goals cannot be met contemporaneously with family goals,[10] the person is very likely to turn a deaf ear to those who want to enrich family life by changing patterns to make them consistent with goals. The question, "What's in it for me?" gets a resounding "NOTHING!!" in response. On the other hand, if members' goals are in harmony and personal growth is compatible with family growth, the family members will be more willing to take the necessary steps toward correction.

Related to this is the degree of commitment that family members feel. I have attempted to indicate that change is problematic and that being willing to correct

[9]   Jack   R.   Gibb,   "Defensive   Communication",   Journal of
       Communication, 11, 1961, pp. 141-148.
[10]   Rosenstock and Kutner, op. cit.

inappropriateness is to be willing to forego pleasure. This takes commitment.

To have sufficient commitment to make the corrective effort is one thing, to have the time and energy to negotiate differences in the definitions of both problem and solution is something else. The harried housewife-mother, the driven businessman, the young couple struggling to pay for a $60,000 house, two cars, furniture, appliances and, at the same time, coordinate the complicated time schedules of husband, wife, children and baby sitter may not have the time and energy resources to expend on reaching consensus. Their inability to share precludes pattern rectification. They may simply have to put up with inappropriateness and recurrent stressors until they reach the point when they are able to talk about correcting the situation. It may be that they self-destruct before this point is reached. This is especially true of those families at the bottom of the social heap. Getting enough to wear and eat and arranging for even minimal accommodations may take so much time and energy that working toward a pleasant family situation is impossible and even the idea is an irrelevant luxury.

Being able to share the definition also depends on the family's success in previous crisis. In families in which sharing previously paid off with a more rewarding family life, it is easier for the sharing to take place for the resulting changes in other definitions (of self, of family, of others) are more likely to be seen as valuable. If nothing exists in the family's history that indicates that a change in one's definitions will be rewarding, the sharing of definitions concerning the problem will be difficult indeed.

And finally, here is the last of the ways that interaction lessens sharing possibilities. Being able to share the definition depends on ". . . the mechanisms employed in previous definitions of events."[12] In short, a family's ability to share is directly related to its member's ability to trust. There must be trust that others will continue to be there, trust that one's interests are considered important by other family members, and trust that an honest attempt is being made to solve the problem. The building and maintaining of trust lends support to sharing the problem's definition. When a family has arrived at this consensus, they have accomplished the first step in their adjustment to crisis.

What family members share is a particular definition of inadequacy; this sharing is made difficult by the problem's

---

[12] Hill, "Generic Features of Families under Stress", op. cit., p. 144.

complexity as well as by the just-mentioned patterns.
Families sometimes have difficulty determining what it is
that is amiss. Frequently, the stressor does not clearly
specify the problem and it must be interpreted before the
inappropriate pattern can be correctly identified. At times,
it is difficult to differentiate between problem and
symptom. That this differentiation of problem and symptom is
difficult has been made amply clear in the literature[13] and
in Chapter 3 above. The family's sharing of an incorrect
definition is not helpful and will result in its later
taking either an Exit or the Repeat Loop. A similar
difficulty exists when the source of the problem is seen as
being either interactional or transactional when really the
source is either not as defined or indeterminate.

Sharing the definition is made difficult if the
stressor confuses the issue so that each person perceives
the other as the source of the difficulty. Earlier,
defensiveness was seen as arising from interaction patterns;
it is also the result of an incorrect perception of the
problem. As long as each person labels the other as the
difficulty's source, the use of Exit 1 is virtually
guaranteed. For example, a stressor has indicated to the
couple that their expenses exceed their income. The
husband's self image requires that he reject his wife's
definition of him as an inadequate breadwinner. Her self
image will not allow her to accept his definition of her as
a spendthrift. The sharing of a definition is rendered
virtually impossible if a loss of face is a concomitant. The
family in this stage must reach an agreement that they have
a particular problem and that something should be done about
it.

Consensus concerning the solution. Once the family has
made a decision about the problem, their next task is to
reach agreement on the solution. The family must agree to a
particular activity that will establish a workable pattern
to replace the one that has been shown to be inappropriate.
Since the solution is based on the preceding agreement about
the problem, if the former definition is inaccurate, the
solution will be wrong and, further down the line,
subsequent action will be irrelevant.

In this part of Secondary Adjustment, as in the
previous part, the family faces the same problem: to arrive

---

[13]   Vogel and Bell, op. cit.; Jules Henry, Pathways to
       Madness (New York: Vintage, 1965) especially pp. 449,
       451; R.D. Laing, A. Esterson, Sanity, Madness and the
       Family (Hammondsworth, Middlesex, England: Penguin,
       1964). Also supporting this idea are therapists such as
       Satir and Minuchin and communications analysts such as
       Haley and Watzlawick.

at consensus. Many of the elements of the previous discussion are relevant here. A family member's vested interest in particular patterns makes reaching censensus difficult, levels of commitment and degrees of trust are crucial to family success, the complexity of family dynamics makes agreement difficult, and the family may have no experience in solving problems of this magnitude. Correction patterns are being employed and since these patterns are general, the family will likely repeat its earlier attempts at consensus.

Agreeing on a solution has special problems because deciding on solution is more difficult than sharing a definition of the problem. Defining the problem is sometimes made easier by the power of the stressor, that is, the problem is somtimes clear. On the other hand, the solution to the problem is rarely obvious and the solution usually requires creative acts. The nature of the problem need only be discovered (and the stressor points the way); the solution must be invented.

Unlike the previous step, reaching agreement about solution has an immediate precedent. For good or ill, the patterns established in arriving at an agreement about the problem will carry over into this phase. This can be advantageous if the prior consensus was reached swiftly, without generating defensiveness. However, if arriving at consensus about the problem was hammered out with difficulty and patterns of indifference or hostility were established, the family will have to deal with those detrimental factors.

During the early stages of the Secondary Adjustment Period one of the family members may volunteer or may be selected to lead the family toward eventual sucess. The existence of a "sponsor" is important. With no sponsor forthcoming, the family is apt to flounder and succumb to the omnipresent pressures to either work on other difficulties or deal with the stressor-related problem at a superficial level. This misplaced attention and action will likely move the family to an exit and back toward uncorrected inappropriateness.

The sponsor may be the family member who was first aware of the stressor or there may be a division of labor and, following the general acceptance of the awareness, some other person may take over the sponsorship of regenerative activity. Sponsorship may be on the basis of greatest personal interest, or prescribed role, or expertise, or past success. The sponsor may volunteer because no one else wants the job. At any rate, success is promoted if a sponsor emerges and directs the family's attention and activity.

Another aspect related to reaching consensus has to do with the generality of the problem and socially prescribed ways of dealing with it. In crisis situations which happen to nearly all families in a given context, society establishes and institutionalizes particular kinds of solutions from which the family need only to choose. Arrival at consensus is accordingly simplified. Death, for example, happens in virtually all families and solutions have been institutionalized. Reaching a solution is almost a mechanical process, however difficult it may be.

At the other extreme are bizarre kinds of occurrences which happen to only one family or only a few families and these instances are so rare that no solutions exist as a part of the culture. The children born with defects whose mothers prenatally ingested thalidomide are a case in point. Interestingly enough, these parents did what might be expected, they came together and helped each other to arrive at the most beneficial solutions.

In between the usual and the rare are the stressors and situations which happen to some families and not to others. The differential in the effect of the first child's entry into the family indicates such a situation. Not only does this differential point to the appropriateness or inappropriateness of the family's patterns, it points to problems in arriving at solution. Families in such a crisis will have to seek out their own solutions because general ones do not exist in the culture and the problem is not rare enought to warrant special attention and the attendant assistance.

If the family cannot reach a solution to the problem it will take Exit 2. If it successfully completes this step, it will move on to the next stage, the stage at which action is taken.

Action. After the family has agreed to a solution, they must take action based on their plan. Until this point, the family's problem has been one of reaching agreement, that is, they have had to make sense out of the world of their experience, share the resulting perception, and devise a plan based on the consensus. Now, action is required and this is another matter. Talking is different from acting and success in the former does not necessarily mean success in the latter. Completing the crisis process as an intact family requires success in both talking and doing; thoughts must be implemented by action or Exit 3 is taken.

"Talk is cheap" goes the saying for talk does not necessarily entail confronting others. Action, on the other hand, is more difficult for it involves other people. This is because actions take place within a system and entail responses from other parts of these systems. The success of the action depends on either the support of the other system parts or the power of the family member to over-ride the negative responses.

There are several systems into which the new behavior must fit. There is the personality system of each family member, the family system itself, and the wider social system. These will be considered in turn.

Action is associated with changes in each family member's self image. This change may be great or small, (its extent depends on the nature of the stressor and the solution to the problem) but some change is required. Behavior and self image reflect each other and a change in one necessitates a change in the other. Since self image involves more than family-related behavior, specific activity will entail a wider image shift. The saying "the spirit is willing, but the flesh is weak", refers to this particular human condition. Unconscious or conscious aspects of personality may preclude a person's participation in a particular solution.

Action requires changes throughout the family system. A problem's successful resolution is facilitated if each family member's activity changes harmoniously with that of the other members. This harmonious change is made difficult if family members are excluded from the decisions of the prior steps. The powerless family members, those not involved in reaching consensus, may be found to be more powerful at this stage, for they can refuse to change and thereby make new patterns difficult to establish. For family success, it is important that members change together and in the same direction.

Finally, there are those outside the family who have transactions with family members. In-laws, employers, close friends, school personnel and the like, must all deal with the family's changed behavior. Changes in family members' behavior necessitate change in the behavior and thinking of non-family members and since these others realize little or no gain from the change, they are slow and unwilling to modify their behavior. Inertia results as the outsiders' reaction slows the changes taking place in the family members. This in turn is carried back into the family and slows the change of the other family members. Since families are open systems, information[14] is passed back and forth between it and other systems. If the other systems indicate

_____

[14] The term "information" includes not only ideas, but behavior as well. Behavior defines the relationship between system units and thereby informs people of the nature of interaction. Behavior can either suggest a shift in the relationship or strengthen whatever exists. In the sense of this current discussion, the family member's behavior suggests a shift while that of the non-family member holds to the previous state of the interaction.

that a change is uncalled for, family change will be inhibited.

When the family makes an attempt to change its patterns or behavior, it has taken a giant step. Even if the attempted change is not correct, the attempt itself sets the scene for a second or third try. These additional attempts are shown on Figure V by the Repeat Loop which is taken after a corrected pattern does not work. This loop moves the family back to a former position within the Secondary Adjustment Period; families regress to the point where the adjustment process went wrong.

If the family's action is totally appropriate, it will move toward restructuring as Secondary Adjustment has been accomplished. Usually, however, other attempts are required. These attempts are facilitated by the initial try which shakes loose the family's every-day procedures. Habitual behavior is rendered conscious, structured ways of perceiving family members become no longer sacrosant, and established patterns are recognized as convention and therefore violable. The result is an opportunity to implement more appropriate response; the inertia of long standing processes has been countered.

Appropriate action. The last step in the Secondary Adjustment Period is the taking of appropriate action. Families who take action and who are able to keep trying will eventually correct their inappropriate patterns. It is the correction of inappropriateness that is the object of this step and the family has acted appropriately when it has thoughtfully and accurately applied its patterns of correction to a difficult situation and it has acted and resolved its initial difficulty.

Generally, the problem will be resolved in two different ways and either way is indicative of high level problem solving skills. One way (Routes B and C1 on Figure V) involves restructuring with a new personnel; the other way (Routes C2 and D) entails the family's continuation with the same adult membership. These different ways will now be explained and more information is provided in Chapter 5.

If, after successfully completing the Secondary Adjustment Period, the family chooses to separate (Route B) as the best solution to its inappropriateness, this can be an indication of strength rather than weakness. Weakness in separation is indicated when the family moves toward separation before completing the steps of Secondary Adjustment. This is Route A and reflects a drift and an inability to successfully resolve the problem. With Route B, however, the family consciously chooses dissolution as the best response to an insolvable difficulty. The family has carefully considered why this is the best response, they are aware of themselves, each other, and the images held by

70

family members. They know about the inappropriateness of their behavior and why they could not correct it. With this information, their separation is a proper solution to resolving the necessity to change and the impossibility to do so. As opposed to Route A, separation after the Secondary Adjustment Period means that important lessons have been learned.

Route C is taken by those families who are required by circumstances to change their personnel. They have "chosen" to restructure themselves with fewer people because the situation is such that they must. Their appropriate action may follow a predictable stressor (an older adolescent leaving home) or an unpredictable one (the death of a family member). In either kind of situation, the family goes through the steps of Secondary Adjustment and eventually moves toward restructuring. Obviously, the death of a family member requires different family activity than does an adolescent's leaving home. Because of the difference, Route C is divided into two paths: C1 which includes families who have lost an adult member, and C2, those families who are being reorganized as the result of a younger family member's departure.

Families can also take Route D and emerge from the Secondary Adjustment Period as an intact unit. Generally, these are stronger families than when they entered the crisis process. They should be more highly integrated for bonds develop as the result of successfully completed tasks. The bonds grow from the sharing of a difficult experience, from their cooperative activity, from completing a task, from indications of their personal worth, and from family harmony. Their ability to solve a problem has been proven and they should feel good about themselves as a group. Patterns have been added to their behavioral repertoire and their patterns of correction have been strengthened. Since the patterns of the Secondary Adjustment Period are essentially the same as those used for correction prior to the stressor, their actions during subsequent Periods of Incipience should become more appropriate and they may be now more able to correct problems before some stressor forces them to.

With the implementation of appropriate action, the family completes the Secondary Adjustment Period. It now moves to Reorganization which involves the solving of other problems within the system, these other difficulties having been created by changes in family process. Before examining Reorganization, a review of the foregoing part of crisis is in order. This review will include a new way of looking at crisis.

FAMILY STRENGTHS

A family's "success" in the Secondary Adjustment Period is related to the degree in which the family accomplishes the steps of secondary adjustment, that is, its effectiveness in progressing to the point of taking appropriate action and moving to Reorganization while keeping to a minimum such negative by-products as resentment, exploitation, force, and personal and family dysfunction. This success is positively related to:

1. High levels of integration and instrumentality.

2. High levels of consistency and flexibility.

3. The speed with which it progresses to the appropriate action step.

4. Prior success with Stressors.

   A. In previous Secondary Adjustment Periods.
   B. In this one.

5. Members' commitment to the family.

6. The existence of a sponsor.

7. The family's support for and acceptance of family members.

8. The family's available energy.

9. Its level of awareness. The family's success depends on:

   A. The number of members who are aware.
   B. The level of acceptance of the aware person.

10. Its success in reaching consensus as to the problem, this being affected by:

    A. Members' ability to exchange ideas.
    B. The felt urgency of reaching agreement.
    C. The family position of the aware person.
    D. The stressor's constancy, force, and the directness between stressor and problem.

11. Reaching consensus about the problem's solution is related to:

    A. The family's success in the previous step.
    B. The same A. through D. of the previous step.
    C. Its ability in inventing solutions.

12.   Taking action depends upon the family's:

A. Being an open system in a helpful environment.
B. Being closed in a hostile environment.
C. Goal commonality of members.
D. Acceptance of risk taking.
E. Tolerance of inconsistency and inefficiency.

13.   Taking appropriate action depends upon:

A. Members' acceptance of the action as being the best response.
B. The action's effectiveness in meeting needs at all relevant levels.
C. The goodness of fit between action and problem.

REVIEW: A NEW LOOK AT FAMILY CRISIS

This review will serve two purposes: first, to provide a breather so that previously presented material can be carefully considered and otherwise digested, and, secondly, to provide a view of the crisis process from a different vantage point.

In this review, the object is to see, in a new light the following: the family's inability to avoid stressors, the importance of the stressor in precipitating a major change in the family's patterns, the difficulty that families have in developing new patterns, and, finally, to begin to understand the difficulties that exist in reorganization. In short, to consider again, the crisis process.

In order to accomplish these four objectives, we will summarily deal with "homeostasis" as a useable term and then, in a much more deliberate manner, consider levels of family functioning and orders of change. With this back-ground information and the new insights it provides, we will re-examine families and deal, in turn, with each of the four objectives that were stated in the preceding paragraph.

Watzlawick suggests that the term "homeostasis" be dropped because of its lack of clarity and he indicates that its two meanings be taken over by the terms "stability" and "negative feedback loops". Stability should be used to refer to the system's "certain constancy" and negative feedback loops[15] should be used to refer to the mechanisms that are used to maintain that constancy.[16] I will follow this suggestion.

Levels of Family Functioning

The following section focuses on levels of family interaction and suggests why the existence of these levels complicates and slows pattern revision during the crisis process. The explanation is complex and understanding is facilitated by dividing the consideration into a series of small steps. The first step is the discussion of levels as universal phenomenon, existing in both theory and reality. Secondly, we will consider levels as they relate to values and associated behavior. Changes in values and behavior will next be considered and the processes associated with change, feedback loops and orders of change, will be the third and final topic. We can then consider the Review and accomplish our four objectives.

The idea of levels is an extremely important one and, at the same time, it is one that students find particularly difficult. I think this difficulty can be lessened if persons will consider what they already know about levels and what has been previously said or implied in this book. We can then move into new areas of applying the idea and arrive at a higher level of understanding.

Level. As the initial approach to understanding levels, think of the words "animal" and "dog". "Animal" is a class and it is more general and less concise than is "dog" as it includes members who are not dogs. Clearly, it is at a different level of abstraction. "Cat" and "tiger" and "ant" are at the same level as "dog"; they are categories within the class of animals.

Consider the education institution. It has a hierarchy which consists of school board, principals, teachers, and students. The teachers are responsible for what goes on in the class room and they answer to the principals who answer to the superintendent who answers to the school board. If something goes wrong in the class room, say a serious student-teacher discipline problem, the principal is the one

---

[15] "Negative" in this context is descriptive rather than evaluative. Negative feedback is different from a negative feedback loop. The former refers to information given to a person about their poor performance. A negative feedback loop, on the other hand, is a family process by which system stability is maintained.

[16] Paul Watzlawick, Janet Helmick Beavin, and Don .D. Jackson, Pragmatics of Human Communication (New York: Norton, 1967), p. 146.

who is called upon to straighten it out. Students are not called upon because they are either uninvolved or part of the problem. Other teachers are not formally involved because it is not their responsibility to see that other teachers' classrooms are working correctly. The superintendent, having an over-seeing function, will only become involved if the situation becomes so damaging that the working of the school system is being upset. So, it is the principal, the person at the next highest level, who steps in to make correction.

If this is understood, then it should be apparent that one way of looking at levels is to see them as a hierarchy. A related way is to consider that behavior at one level affects, or fixes, or considers, or directs behavior at some other level. The first paragraph of this section, the one starting with "The idea of levels is an extremely important one," is at a different level than the paragraph you just read. The first paragraph indicated what was going to happen and the second paragraph was that which happened. In interaction, a family communicates and when family members talk about a family event they are talking about communication. This communication about communication, called metacommunication, is different from communication. Since it looks back at communication and it is the means by which communication is thought about and discussed, metacommunication is at a different logical level.

In this book we have previously considered levels. Correction patterns, in that they are the means by which execution patterns are made appropriate, are at a different level than the execution patterns. I also noted that a difficulty can be turned into a problem if the action taken does not accurately reflect the problem's seriousness. Put into the terms of the present discussion, problems are created when action is taken at the wrong level. The explanation associated with the Period of Incipience deals exhaustively with this issue.

One additional consideration: families are complex groups. On the one hand a family is a unit with a life that begins, continues, and ends. On the other hand, a family is composed of individuals who live only a part of the time in the family. Both the individual and the family are capable of maintaining an independent existence. This indicates the existence of two levels of a family, the group level and the individual level.

So much for levels they are hierarchial and general. To make them more specific, I will apply level ideas to values and associated behavior.

Family values and behavior. The following discussion centers on values. By "values" I mean the criteria which are used to judge the worth of some behavior or thought. We call upon certain values when we establish priorities, make comparisons, establish goals, or judge behavior.

Values are usually thought of as being a property of an individual. But, there is a sense in which a family has values. A family's values emerge when each member's values are mixed with those of every other member. The mix of values is a singular one for no two families order their values the same way. One family may hold its unity to be more important than the growth of its individual members. Another will put individual growth first. Whichever the case, a value hierarchy results.

To speak of the ordering of values is to imply boss values, those higher order values which provide the basis for the order. To say that some value A is more important than some value B is to say that an underlying set of criteria is being used for judgement purposes. This set of criteria is at a different logical level than that to which the criteria are applied. Values related to parenting, to spousal behavior, to dealing with non-family members, to a thousand other family matters, are combined in accordance with weights that are idiosyncratically assigned. The weights that the family assigns to its values reflect its higher order values. For example, the belief that physical abuse should not be a part of family life is a reflection of higher order values in the areas of human dignity and the rights of women and children.

Values do not exist in isolation, they are manifested in behavior. Just as values form a hierarchy, so does the related behavior. For example, a family highly regards family unity and accordingly stays together. At another level, it positively evaluates financial security because that supports family unity. It then takes action to establish and maintain solvency. Decisions about saving money are made in terms of the higher order values and the specific activity of saving reflects the decisions. An example of a value hierarchy is:

Level	The Value	The Behavior
Most Basic	Unity is most important	Staying Together
Intermediate	Financial security is important as it supports unity and is important in its own right	The establishment of financial security and the maintenance of solvency
Primary	Saving money is good for it supports family unity and solvency	Saving money

A family's way of life is a manifestation of its value structure; its behavior expresses its values. The family's organization (its rules, its interaction patterns, its transactions with non-family people) reflects its values.

Generally, there exists a congruency between values and behavior and a change in values will have the tendency to change behavior. It works the other way as well, for a change in behavior will have the tendency to change the related values. When behavior changes, it expresses a different value. To the degree that the new behavior persists, the old value will lose meaning. Example: if a parent physically abuses a child for some behavior for which the child was not previously punished in an abusive way, the old value (that children have dignity) will be challenged. If the abusive punishment is repeated, a new value (that maintaining control is of utmost importance) will become prominent.

The value-behavior hierarchy. In the foregoing section, three levels of values and behavior were indicated. Although there may be other levels, thinking in terms of these three will be sufficient for our purposes. To sensibly talk about levels, we need some categories. Highest-level values (e.g. those associated with unity in the previous example) will be referred to as "basic" values and the associated behavior is the "family's style". At the next level are the "intermediate" values and behavior (e.g. the values and behavior associated with financial security). At the most immediate and specific level will be found "surface" values and behavior (e.g. behavior and values associated with saving money).

The basic values are the most general and the most diffuse of the family's values. They are virtually never discussed and the family may not even be consciously aware of them. These values are part of the family's world-taken-for-granted, they are its frame of reference. Families are founded and organized around these basic ideas.

Basic values are so general that they are rarely directly manifested in observable behavior; their manifestation is usually at the intermediate and primary levels. One exception to this is that the family's continued integration reflects its high evaluation of unity. Basic values are important because they determine the ordering of intermediate values. This ordering results in a unique combination of acceptable behavior and this unique combination is the family's life style. The life style, then, is the behavioral manifestation of its basic values; it is the expression of its basic values. Cuber and

Harroff[17] classify families as either passive-congenial, conflict habituated, devitalized, vital, or total. This classification is of the family's style, its behavior at the most general level.

Intermediate values are less general than basic values. The intermediate values are subject to more explicit consideration by family members. Yet, consideration is rare even at this level and is most likely to occur during the formative part of the relationship and in times of stress. Intermediate values concern the most desirable:

A. Family organization; authoritarian, democratic or anarchic.

B. Level of commitment.

C. Degree of separateness and connectedness; the degree to which there should be sharing of different spaces: emotional, geographic, time, sexual, ideological, and experiential; decisions concerning personal autonomy.

D. Degree of consensus among family members concerning themselves, each other, and the family.

E. Strength of boundaries between that which is family and that which is not.[18]

The intermediate level is the bridge between basic values and the primary behavior. Basic values are involved when families make decisions at the intermediate level; particular behavior at the primary level is called for because of the decision that is made. If a family decides on an authoritarian structure, both the relative power of husband and wife vis-a-vis each other and their parental power vis-a-vis their children will be framed and the family government as practised will fit the frame.

Surface behavior is the action component of the values at the higher levels with which it is consistent. Although there are surface values, it is surface behavior which is a

---

[17] John F. Cuber and Peggy B. Harroff, Sex and the Significant Americans (Baltimore: Penguin Books, 1965), pp. 43-65.

[18] I have used material from Hess and Handel as a basis for this particular section. Their analysis was not directly applicable so I have modeled it to fit my needs. Robert D. Hess and Gerald Handel, "The Family as a Psychosocial Organization," The Psychosocial Interior of the Family, (ed.) Gerald Handel (Chicago: Aldine, 1967), pp. 10-24.

more important consideration because of its existence as the day-to-day expression of the family's higher level values. Consider the following actions. These surface level behaviors reflect intermediate values, the values on the preceding list that bear the same letter designation.

A. Forming coalitions, allowing or preventing certain kinds of behavior; coercing or convincing as a means of parental control; being spontaneous or formal.

B. Investing or witholding time, energy, financial resources.

C. Being contentious or harmonious, acting cooperatively or competitively, maintaining distance or drawing near.

D. Exchanging testimony, communicating about self and others, testing, affirming, disqualifying, rejecting, diverging.

E. The composing of the family; the sharing of the family secrets, the sharing of the family's space, time, energy and money.

I have shown that there is a hierarchy of values and related behavior. What is most important is that when behavior occurs it reflects a particular value. If the value it reflects is one that has been accepted by the family, the family's way of life is reinforced. If the behavior reflects a value which is not part of the family's culture, the family's way of life is put in question. Negotiation then takes place and the new value-behavior is either accepted or rejected.

And now, we get to the heart of the matter. Commonly, behavior at one level is performed and negotiated in such a way that values at the next higher level are not affected. Usually, surface behavior, either singularly or in combination, supports higher level values. The surface behavior patterns, those on the preceding list, are the material out of which Jackson's homeostatic devices,[19] Speer's morphostatic devices,[20] and negative feedback loops are constructed. Before considering change and inertia, lets consider an example.

An example. Most of the surface level patterns that I have listed are generalities, they are not specific and identifiable behaviors. The number of specific behaviors

---

[19]   See footnote 4, Chapter 1.
[20]   Speer, op. cit., pp. 249, 278.

that can be employed to express an intermediate value is immense and we can only mention a few. Since families deal with jointly gained, held, and expended resources of time, energy, space, money and things, specific surface behaviors can be classified in those areas. In the following, one selected intermediate value, the balance of separateness and connectedness, is considered in terms of its related behavior.

Values held by each spouse: That personal freedom is very important and the expectations of others are largely unwarranted attacks on personal autonomy.

The basic value: A family should allow much autonomy so that each member can live a largely unrestricted life.

The intermediate value: Families should have open roles; separateness is to be more highly regarded than connectedness.

Surface level behavior:

Space: A minimum of space sharing.
- Private rooms or spaces where others are admitted by invitation only.
- Knocking before entering closed rooms.
- Furniture arrangement placed to promote individual activities such as reading rather than group activities such as game playing or talking.
- Wide spaces, or reading, or quietness during joint activities such as eating.
- Spending vacations in separate locations.
- Working away from home and each other.
- Dancing with a minimum of touching and mutual movement.

Time: A minimum of time sharing.
- Going to bed at separate times and arising separately.
- Eating meals at different times.
- She does the shopping while he tends the yard.
- Frequent non-punctuality.

Energy: A minimum of joint activities.
- He skis and she curls.
- Never are they bridge partners.
- She cooks and he reads the paper.
- He works on the car as a hobby while she sews.
- He has friends and interests that she does not share and vice versa.

80

Money, things:
- They each have separate bank and charge
  accounts.
- He locks his tool box.
- She secures her purse.
- They each have an automobile which they
  frequently drive to the same location.
- She buys her clothes and he buys his without any
  mutual consultation.

The list of behaviors associated with any intermediate
value is virtually endless. The surface behaviors are
consistent with each other and they affirm, in this case,
the level of individuation that each family member will
have.

So far in this review, we have considered levels,
levels of values, and the relationship between values and
behavior. With this background we can move on to the major
concern of the model and the chapter: change and family
pattern persistence. First, we will consider problems
associated with maintaining stability and then discuss
change processes and orders of change. This will take us to
the consideration of the four issues which is the goal of
this section.

Change and Inertial Levels of Values and Behavior

Family dynamics can be tricky at times because
stability and change are perpetually in process and mutually
impacting. In this section, I will explore this mutual
impact and the processes that are related.

Stability as a problem. In the last section, I
attempted to show how a family's behavior expresses its
values relative to some dimension of family interactional
life. On each dimension a balance is processed. When members
feel comfortable with the balance, that is when it is
congruent with their values, they affirm the status quo with
their behavior.

If life were simple, a person could imagine that a
given level of relationship could be maintained by constant
affirmation. That is, once a satisfactory balance was
achieved between, say, closeness and separateness,
interactional affirmation of that balance should provide
comfortable stability.

Unfortunately, such simplicity is unreal because life
is more complicated than that. With affirmation, there is
stability but the stability is short lived. Stability is
brief because constant affirmation tends to change the
value. In the example in the previous section, constant
affirmation of separateness will tend to increase the social
distance. In order to keep within agreed-upon limits,

closeness must be sometimes incorporated into interaction patterns. At the surface level, some behavior which promotes closeness will occur which will counter the process of individuation and thereby maintain stability at the intermediate level. The important idea is that patterns of closeness and separateness are both necessary. Put more generally, the maintenance of any interactional balance requires the incorporation of "extreme" behavior. The point is not that extreme behavior is essential, the point is that a balance, which is somewhere in the middle on some dimension, is maintained by behavior which comes from both ends of the dimension's continuum.

Stability of a family's values and behavior is also affected by change in individual family members. Since the family is at one level and its members are at another, a person can change either his mind or heart and place an agreed-upon value in question. When this happens, the family's value must change or the person's value must change or the family will tend to move apart. There is one other possibility: the family's continued existence with intramural competing value systems. The resulting confusion is difficult for most families to handle so this is usually a temporary situation. In any case, the family is not in a stable state.

Given the opportunity, families will always change their more immediate behavior to maintain stability of their higher level values. They will revise surface behavior before intermediate values and, before changing basic values, they will change at the intermediate level. Families do not want to change at all and if change is required they will take the route of smallest revision. Haley's first law is "When one person indicates a change in relation to another, the other will act upon the first so as to diminish and modify that change."[21] In this case, families act as they have in the past and they attempt to make the smallest possible change.

The greater the change, the more disruption of patterns, confusion of affect, and inefficiency in task performance. These are not enviable states and, since families are formed to provide the opposites, people attempt to hold to pattern consistency, steady affect, and efficiency rather than to undergo change.

The higher the level of the value that is changed, the more revision is necessary in the family. This is because the more general values affect behavior and values at all the more immediate levels. A change in surface behavior will

---

[21]   Jay Haley, Strategies of Psychotherapy (New York: Grunes & Stratton, 1963), p. 189.

usually be neutralized by a change in some other surface behavior and intermediate values are not necessarily affected. On the other hand, if intermediate values change, the related surface values and behavior will necessarily change.

In the preceding, we have seen how a family has values and behavior that are at different levels. The other important idea is that values at one level are supported by behavior at the next most specific and immediate level. In the following section, we will explore the processes by which stability and change are accomplished.

Feedback loops. Behavior that promotes family stability, that reduces deviation, is called a negative feedback loop. These loops are called "negative" because they include some input which is the opposite of some other formerly introduced input and the latter NEGATES the effect of the former. The result is the system's overall stability. When some behavior at the surface level engenders uneasiness in the family, that is, when it is incongruent with an intermediate value to such a degree that the value is disputed, the family will counter the doubt-producing activity with behavior which is its opposite. The new behavior will tend to neutralize the initial activity and the questioned intermediate value will remain unchanged. By using negative feedback loops, a family can make minor changes and no major change will occur in the family system at that time.

An example of a negative feedback loop. In a parent-child relationship, the punishment of the child by the parent usually increases cross-generational distance. The parent who later goes out of his way to indicate his concern for the child counters the distance-creating effect of punishment. If the child accepts the parent's move, the family's agreed level of closeness is maintained.

Just as important as the negative feedback loops are the positive feedback loops. These loops do not minimize deviation in the system as do negative feedback loops; they amplify deviation. Using the same example, if the child feels comfortable with the distance created by the punishment (this might be the case if the child is maturing and is looking for a way to leave) he will not move closer as a result of the parent's show of concern. If the child rejects the overture it is likely that the parent will take this as a rejection of himself and, in turn, might reject the child. A self-supporting circle of interaction will have begun and the result will be increased distance until a new organization of parent-child interaction has been established. The intermediate value will then have been revised.

Said in another way, the major difference between

83

positive and negative feedback loops is in the way the parts of these loops work together. Negative feedback loops contain contrary elements which counter-balance each other. The result is that, although there is change within the system, the system itself does not change. Positive feedback loops do not have these countervailing elements which produce balance. Instead, the change of one component is accentuated by some change in another component. With positive feedback loops, it is as though the system takes off; there is no governor that keeps it under control. This eventually results in a change of the system, not merely a change within the system.

Both kinds of loops are essential for family health. A viable family has patterns which provide it with continuity and stability (negative loops) and it has other patterns which promote adaptability (positive loops).

Orders of change. There are different kinds of change. One kind of change, generally associated with a negative feedback loop, is called first order change. With this kind of change, behaviors change at one level and their changing is such that higher level values remain stable. With this type of change, the system remains the same although, and because, there is change within the system.

The other kind of change is second order change. This occurs when the system itself is revised, that is, when there is a change in the structure, or personnel, or basic values. No negative feedback loops are employed to maintain the status quo; positive feedback loops have thrown the system out of balance. The result is a major change in the family's way of life.

To apply orders of change to family values, basic values are maintained by first order change at the intermediate level and intermediate values are supported by first order change at the surface level. With a second order change, basic level values change because intermediate behaviors do not counteract each other. Also intermediate values change because some surface level behavior is not neutralized but its deviation from the family norm is amplified. This deviation amplification is a positive feedback loop and can be the result of a family's awareness that behavior and values are incongruent and that the values should be revised. It can also be the result of changes in either the family's personnel or in the personnel's relative position. It can also be the result of a stressor event.

Usually, families require a second order change to make a satisfactory recovery from problems generated by inappropriateness. Their previous use of first order change techniques has not only supported inappropriateness, it has entrenched it. That is, the damaging effects of dysfunction at basic levels has temporarily, but only temporarily, been defused by negative feedback loops. These first order change processes have enabled the family to keep going by establishing patterns which accommodate, but do not correct, the inappropriateness. Accommodated, the dysfunction will remain or be later reintroduced and be supported by the associated accommodating patterns. To be free of dysfunction, the family is usually required to change the deep seated source of the problem wherever it is, whether it be in its personnel, its structure, or in its basic values. This usually requires a second order change.

In the preceding, I say "usually" because some families can emerge from crisis with their basic values, structure, and personnel unchanged. Some of these are strong families with sound correction patterns and the stressor is likely to be of the unpredictable kind. Such basic values as the importance of family continuity, the integrity and importance of each family member, the perceived high value of mutual support, high levels of affect, personal responsibility for behavior, and strong and appropriate generational coalitions will assist the family to successfully change. These basic values are appropriate and need no revision. Other families, those for whom danger and hardship are commonplace facts of life may well develop an organization which is adapted to recurrent difficulties. This organization may well remain unchanged because negative feedback loops provide the needed flexibility.

With this background information we are ready to again view the crisis process. We can now deal with the four issues which comprised this review's objective.

The Four Issues Considered

Thus far in this review, I have been concerned with providing background material which would allow students to consider the crisis process from a new perspective, that perspective being related to changes in values and behavior. If I have been successful, we can now consider the four major issues related to family crisis: the family's inability to avoid stressors, the importance of the stressor in precipitating change, the difficulty in establishing new patterns, and the problems associated with family Reorganization. These will be taken in turn.

Inability to avoid stressors. Families organize around their basic values and as they enter the crisis process these values have been supportively implemented at more immediate levels. This support deeply implants the family's values and behavior. As we have seen, some of these established patterns are inappropriate and the family must correct them if it is to avoid a stressor. Using our knowledge of family levels, it should now be more clear why families do not correct the inappropriateness.

85

Families cannot move quickly or accurately to correct their patterns for two basic reasons. In the first place, it is difficult for a family member to know what is wrong because the situation is infused with doubt. Since a person acts in both the family system and his own personality system, it is difficult to keep the systems separate in making analysis. The person cannot know if his perception of problems is tied to the family's need or to his own personality need.

Moreover, each other family member will respond to that which is initiated in terms of his personality and perception. Since family members respond in terms of their own needs and perceptions, it is possible and even likely that the reactor will discount the initial request for change. A great deal of effort must be expended to sort out the requirements of the two levels and the confusion of levels; there must be trust enough to mutually see things in terms of the family system's needs.

The second reason why families have difficulty in correcting their patterns is that families prefer minor changes to major changes. In the typical situation, the family will change at the primary level to avoid changing at the intermediate level. They perceive their problem to be an inadequate inplementation of an appropriate value rather than a congruent manifestation of an inappropriate value. Change at the wrong level usually fails to bring about the necessary revision. The dysfunction continues to exist and, being left untreated, it has the tendency to intensify.

An element of confusion is added to the situation at this point for the lower level change sometimes appears to have solved the problem. Remedial activity, even at the wrong level, sometimes mitigates the problem because the taking of action indicates concern and commitment. These are positively evaluated by family members and the good feelings that are generated make those involved feel that progress is being made. This may bode well for future attempts at correction but it is false hope in terms of solving their immediate inappropriateness.

Moreover, wrong level revision may be momentarily helpful in that drastic behavior is balanced with other behavior and the minimization of the effect of the drastic behavior is taken as evidence that the problem is solved. Again, unless change takes place at the correct level, at the highest level of dysfunction, the family will move inexorably toward the stressor.

As an example of the confounding effect of wrong-level change, we could well consider alcoholism. First of all, a person's excessive drinking can be seen as a wrong-level solution. In many cases, a person with some difficulty that can neither be resolved nor lived with reduces the attendant pain by drinking. Of course, this solution is not satisfactory as the source of the pain, the initial difficulty, is unaffected and continues to generate discomfort. A right-level action would attend to the pain-generating-difficulty not to the pain. In time, with continued pain and ineffective attempts at solution, the addictive qualities of alcohol will take over and the initial difficulty will become a major problem.

Let's consider the alcoholic in a family setting with his/her felt pain emanating from family interaction. Dealing with the alcoholic without considering the family context is another instance of a wrong-level solution. Therapy applied solely to the alcoholic will be, at best, only temporarily effective because, even if "cured", the alcoholic will again be subject to the same interaction patterns which exist unchanged. Despite the best of intentions, the drinker may be unable to deal with the painful patterns while sober. Thus, the "chronic" nature of alcoholism. A right-level solution would attempt to correct the pain-generating family interaction <u>and</u> the inability of the family unit to correct the painful situation. Another goal of therapy would be, of course, the reduction of alcohol consumption.

Finally, the alcoholic's promise to stay sober is another instance of a wrong level solution. A promise only makes sense, can only be kept if what is promised can be accomplished by an act of will. Sobriety is not a matter of a person's willing themself to self-control. Inebriety is not the result of a lack of will-power. In fact, as Bateson powerfully indicated, the success of Alcoholics Anonymous is based on the idea that the first step to fighting addiction is the recognition and admission that one is powerless against the drug.[22] At any rate, a promise to maintain sobriety is not to be believed because a promise comes from the person's consciousness which is not the source of the problematic behavior.

As exemplified by the family with an alcoholic, we can see why families find it difficult to change their patterns. Inappropriateness continues because families cannot tell what is amiss. This inappropriateness unequally affects family members and requires that some change more than others and change is usually associated with discomfort. To remove inappropriateness, families must correct their patterns at the right level and this level is usually more basic than they are accustomed to think about and they prefer to change their more immediate surface behavior.

---

[22]   Bateson, <u>op</u>. <u>cit</u>., p. 313.

<u>Importance</u> <u>of</u> <u>the</u> <u>stressor</u> <u>in</u> <u>precipitating</u> <u>change</u>. As the
family continues its wrong level correction, the
inappropriateness becomes entrenched and buttressed by an
increasing number of supporting lower level values. This
state of affairs continues until the dysfunction becomes too
pronounced and the situation explodes. It usually takes a
major event, a stressor, to jolt the family to the point
where change is possible.

The explosion can take many forms and the effect may be
far removed from the problem. Lederer and Jackson,[23] Bell
and Vogel[24] are but four of the authors who discuss how
tension is passed through the family network to emerge in
some seemingly unrelated phenomenon. Tension that has its
source in a family member's transactions can erupt in an
interactional pattern as well as in some transactional
pattern. Interaction difficulties at one level, say at the
spouse level, can emerge elsewhere internally, as in the
case of some kinds of adolescent misbehavior.

Regardless of source, one function of the stressor
(especially a predictable one) is to destroy one of the
family's myths. All families generate myths, myths about
what the family is like, myths about what the family members
are like. In ably functioning families these myths are
generally benign but in dysfunctional families the myths are
likely to be malignant. In the case of malignancy, the myths
justify or maintain inappropriateness. Whether the myth is
"everyone in our family is treated equally well" or "my
husband and I love each other" or "Everything would be all
right if it wasn't for her", the myth at whatever level can
no longer be believed. Although the myth may have been
around for years, its day has passed. The destruction of a
myth of interaction points directly to problems for which
the family must take responsibility.

The destruction of the myth occurs because of the
existence of different system levels. The existence of
personal systems within the family system is one source: not
all family members benefit equally from a myth. An
integration-supportive myth may be destroyed when the person
who "everything would be all right except for" matures
and/or gets outside support and rebels. This rebellion will
be a stressor, the rebel being no longer convinced that the
family's continuation is worth the price she must pay.

System levels are again involved when other
institutions are aware of the family's myth and the related
failure to meet its social responsibilities. The family as
an open system must transact with other institutions. Either

---

[23] Lederer and Jackson, <u>op</u>. <u>cit</u>.
[24] Vogel and Bell, <u>op</u>. <u>cit</u>.

the school that must deal with the acting-out adolescent or the bank that does not get the monthly payment may be the agency of stress. These and other outside institutions know when the family is not working properly and they usually do not hesitate to let the family know of their appraisal. A stressor results.

The stressor has another important effect on the family. In the confusion that surrounds a stressor, some family members can exert more power than they usually do. This power can be within the family or it can be in terms of individual freedom. An example of the former is a wife's taking over the finances with a husband's incapacitation. An example of the latter would be a young person's taking advantage of family confusion to extricate himself from enmeshment and, by leaving home, take first steps toward the liberation of his personality and the self-direction of his life.

The stressor provides the family with this information: Your attempts to revise the situation have been incorrect. They have not worked and the inappropriateness has intensified. There is something essentially wrong and the viability of the family requires that the basic problem be corrected. No more primary change, it is a waste; now, try intermediate change. First order change does not work, second order change is needed. In other words, the stressor ends the period of the crisis process when negative feedback loops characterize its behavior. During secondary adjustment a positive feedback loop characterizes effectively functioning families.

Difficulty in establishing new patterns. The family has difficulty in thinking in terms of major change. After all, if change at the intermediate level had been obviously needed and easy to do, the family would have done it long ago. The hard lesson taught by the stressor falls on the family with congruent and entrenched albeit inappropriate patterns.

Before the stressor, family patterns had been related to each other. With the stressor, change of a high level value is indicated and most other values at the same level will need revision as will virtually all lower level values. The correction of the inappropriateness entails the establishment of a new set of harmonious values and behavior and this new harmony will affect all the family members.

In its attempt to establish new and correct patterns, a family has a difficult job. Drawing again on Watzlawick,[25] there is the possibility that the family itself has added to

---

[25] Watzlawick, et al., Change, op. cit.

its own problems through their former mishandling of some
difficulty. Their inappropriate attempts at correction have
not only failed to resolve the initial difficulty, they have
exacerbated it and now the family must deal with problems
associated with non-correction as well as with the original
difficulty.

In the terms of this model, an inappropriate execution
pattern has been mishandled and the family's inappropriate
correction patterns have made the problem that much worse.
The family is now faced with a complex matter. The members
must sort out the initial difficulty from the problem-
intensifying-solution. They must generate a new and correct
solution to the original difficulty without further
upsetting the family; they must discontinue their
ineffective attempts at solution. This is all to be
accomplished in a situation which is highly charged
emotionally and very demanding of the family members' energy
and best mental efforts.

Eventually, the family either moves toward separation
or makes the necessary secondary adjustment. It finds the
appropriate new value and develops lower level behavior
which supports it. The family members accept both the new
values and the related behavior and the family moves into
Reorganization where this new system will be made into the
family's way of life.

Problems in Reorganization. In the Period of
Reorganization, the major task is to rebuild the family
around the new and corrected family system. This means that
the family must handle the problems that are the by-products
of the crisis process. For example, it must reduce the
tension generated by the stressor and by the confusion
resulting from the family's efforts to rearrange their
values and related behavior. Also, the family must see that
its new system is reasonably internally consistent and that
all family members are committed to it. It is these issues
that we turn to in the next chapter.

CHAPTER 5

REORGANIZATION

The family at the beginning of the Reorganization Period is different from what it was during Incipience: major change in the family system has taken place. This, however, is not the end of the crisis period because the process of change, that is, the activity associated with the correction of inappropriateness, entails two additional tasks. These tasks are related to the problems brought about by the crisis process itself; the problems exist regardless of the kind of pattern which was inappropriate or the nature of the stressor. All families in crisis face these tasks and the process is not complete until they have successfully completed them.

In this chapter, we will first consider the two tasks of Reorganization, consolidation and rebounding, and the residues of earlier parts of the crisis process. This will be followed by a detailed consideration of the different kinds of structures which families exhibit as they emerge from Reorganization.

CONSOLIDATION AND REBOUNDING

Consolidation

One of the family's tasks is to achieve a level of consistency in values which will enable it to adequately function. This consistency is of three kinds: first, among the values of each person; second, in the values held by the various family members; third, between existing values and current behavior. The family, at the beginning of the crisis process had general consistency in its values and the associated behavior patterns. Unfortunately for them, this value set included one which was inappropriate; this value was then reflected in inappropriate behavior which the stressor indicated would have to be changed. During Secondary Adjustment, the inappropriateness was corrected, that is, the value and behavior were made appropriate and, with this revision, inconsistency was introduced into the family's value-behavior set. The new value and behavior are not consistent with the values and behaviors which have continued unchanged. During Reorganization, one of the family's tasks is to generate a consistent set of values all of which are reflected in appropriate behavior. Figure VI is a representation of this process.

Period of Incipience	Stressor	Secondary Adjustment Period	Reorganization
A_1 Appropriate		A_1	A_2
B_1 Inappropriate	Impact here	B_2	B_2
C_1 Appropriate		C_1	C_2
D_1 Appropriate		D_1	D_2
All Values Consistent		All Values Appropriate	All Values Appropriate and Consistent
One Is Inappropriate		One is Inconsistent	

Figure VI
Value Consistency and Appropriateness

In the simplistic representation, Figure VI, four
values are indicated (A1, B1, C1, D1) and these are   3454
consistent with each other. Note that B1, although   3455
consistent with the other values, is inappropriate. The   3456
stressor indicates the existence of that inappropriateness   3457
and during Secondary Adjustment the pattern is corrected.   3458
The value is now labeled B2 to reflect the change. The other 3459
values carry the subscript "1" to indicate their sameness   3460
over time. B2 as changed provides the family with totally   3461
appropriate patterns but the change has upset the prior   3462
value consistency. During Reorganization, the other values   3463
(A, C, and D) must be changed so that a new consistency can 3464
be established. This consistency, to be lasting and   3465
satisfying, must include only appropriate values.   3466

In short, the new value and behavior must be   3467
incorporated into the family system and this is accomplished
by changing inconsistent values to make them consistent with 3468
the newly appropriate one. Consolidation is the process of   3469
constructing an appropriate and consistent set of values.   3470

Following Spiegal's lead, I call this "consolidation".   3472
As he put it:

Consolidating is the last step. It is   3475
required because the compromise solution is
characterized by novelty, and cognitive strain is   3476
still present. Even though ego and alter establish
a compromise, they must still learn how to make it   3477
work. To put the matter somewhat differently,
compromise can be defined as the adjustment and   3478
redistribution of rewards. The roles are modified

92

through the redistribution of goals. The new roles
still have to be worked through and internalized
by ego and alter as they discover how to reward
each other in playing the new roles.[1]

Consolidating is the making consistent of the family's
patterns.

Rebounding

The family's other task is to bounce back, to rebound.
The crisis process, especially the Stressor and the
Secondary Adjustment Period have shaken the family and its
members. There has been confusion, stress, anxiety and, if
nothing else, tiredness. Family members have focused their
energy on finding the solution to their stressor-related
problem. Other parts of family life have atrophied. Things
have not been said and have not been done so levels of
integration have suffered and instrumentality has been
reduced. The family needs to rebound to a high level of
integration and effective problem solving. It needs to
achieve a new dynamic equilibrium and this can only be done
if the tangential problems created by earlier difficulties
are resolved. Rebounding is the reintegration of the family
by dealing with the problems brought about by the process of
change.

Consider this example in terms of consolidating and
rebounding actions. Imagine a family in which appropriate
patterns grew in a context in which the wife's lack of
personhood and the husband's need to dominate resulted in

---

[1]   John P. Spiegal, "The Resolution of Role Conflict Within
the Family," The Patient and the Mental Hospital, (eds.)
Milton Greenblatt, D.J. Levinson, R.H. Williams
(Glencoe: The Free Press, 1957). Interestingly enough
Spiegal states in this important article: "I have
distinguished eleven steps in the process (re-
equilibration) which I will here describe briefly. I
believe these steps have a temporal order and that this
order has a kind of internal logic. Unfortunately, I am
unable to discern the basis of the order and must
therefore leave the presentation in an excessively
descriptive and ad hoc condition". (emphasis mine.) The
eleven steps he indicates are coercion, coaxing,
evaluating, masking, postponing, role reversal, joking,
referral to a third party, exploring, compromising and
consolidating. The first group of five leads to
unsuccessful problem resolution while the last five are
more effective. Spiegal's inability to perceive an
"internal logic" can now be rectified for the first five
are related to a first order change and the second five
are related to a second order change.

93

her abject submission to him. Her pay-off was being a spendthrift; his was domination. The stressor was the "repossession" of furniture which she purchased on one of her sprees. The Period of Secondary Adjustment ended with changed spousal roles and a job for her; he was relieved of responsibility for her finances and they reorganized as an intact family.

Continuing with the example, consolidation provides for the revision of their other patterns to reflect this new mutuality and maturity. Pattern consistency requires that he be more involved in parenting, that she initiate more discussions and that decisions be made with more sharing. In intimate affairs there would be more concern for her satisfaction and more wife-initiated sexual activity.

In rebounding they would deal with the problems that the entire process created. With a role change this great, both will be confused about the new expectations. In all liklihood, they will be anxious about their ability to act in the new way, for they will be less than sure about their new selves. She may find herself anxious about her ability to do what is now required to do and this anxiety may itself produce inability. He may feel threatened by his wife's new place as an equal opportunity enjoyer and may react defensively. The result is a lower level of integration and a reduction in their ability to accomplish necessary tasks. With successful rebounding, the reduction in both the effectiveness of execution patterns and in the level of integration is only temporary. Rebounding brings higher levels of certainty and the assurance that the new system will work.

Residues

The two major tasks of Reorganization not only grow from the preceding steps of the crisis process but the family's success in Reorganization reflects earlier events. The Reorganization is affected by the stressor and by processes that are a part of Secondary Adjustment. The stressor's impact is important because the more severe the stressor, the more that values and behavior will be changed. This greater change will be in the number of values/behavior that change and also in the degree to which the values and behavior change. A minor stressor will affect just a few values and the effect will be mild.

With a stressor's greater impact, there will be a greater disruption of family functioning. This will result in more unmet needs of family members, less success in meeting social expectations, and less success in the family's meeting its own system requirements. All this points to intensified Reorganization problems as these stem from the stressor's impact.

94

The faster and more directly the family moves through Secondary Adjustment, the fewer will be their problems in rebounding. Speed reduces the liklihood of inappropriateness being generated in other family patterns.[2] It also lessens the possibility that any inappropriateness which might develop would have the chance to become habitual and entrenched.

Speed and directness during Secondary Adjustment will effect the tasks of consolidation because the same correction patterns used during Secondary Adjustment are applicable during Reorganization. Moreover, the bonds that developed and the feelings of success that were engendered will strengthen families and help them through this Reorganization Period.

In summary, families at this point in the crisis process have patterns which are all appropriate (this accomplished during Secondary Adjustment) and values which are all consistent and reflected congruently in behavior (this accomplished during consolidation in Reorganization). During rebounding, members have solved the tangential difficulties so they are again experiencing the priceless unessentials. For the successful families as well as the unsuccessful ones, a number of organizational structures are possible and in the next section we will consider these structures and compare the attendant advantages and disadvantages.

FAMILY TYPES DURING REORGANIZATION

Figure VII Explained

The figure which follows shows the various routes (five in number) to Reorganization. Three of these are taken by families whose revised organization includes different personnel; two routes are taken by intact families whose personnel stays constant (at least the adults) but whose values and behavior patterns change. Those families with different personnel, called modified families, use routes A, B, and C1 on the Figure VII. Routes C2 and D are taken by intact families.

The modified families have a changed personnel.

---

[2]   As Hill said, "Rather fully corroborated within the new contexts of war separation and reunion were the following generalizations from previous studies . . . . . the length of time a family continues to be disorganized as a result of crisis is inversely related to its adequacy of organization." "Genertic Features of Families Under Stress," op. cit., p. 147.

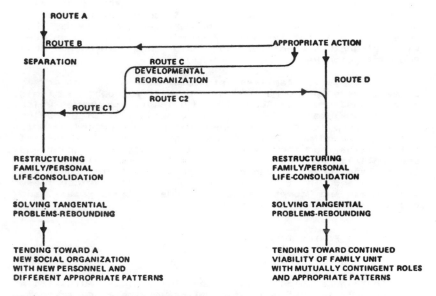

ROUTE A

ROUTE B ← APPROPRIATE ACTION

SEPARATION

ROUTE C
DEVELOPMENTAL
REORGANIZATION

ROUTE D

ROUTE C2

ROUTE C1

RESTRUCTURING
FAMILY/PERSONAL
LIFE-CONSOLIDATION

RESTRUCTURING
FAMILY/PERSONAL
LIFE-CONSOLIDATION

SOLVING TANGENTIAL
PROBLEMS-REBOUNDING

SOLVING TANGENTIAL
PROBLEMS-REBOUNDING

TENDING TOWARD A
NEW SOCIAL ORGANIZATION
WITH NEW PERSONNEL AND
DIFFERENT APPROPRIATE PATTERNS

TENDING TOWARD CONTINUED
VIABILITY OF FAMILY UNIT
WITH MUTUALLY CONTINGENT ROLES
AND APPROPRIATE PATTERNS

Figure VII   REORGANIZATION

Families that take Route A and B are separated families, and
this category includes both separate and divorced units   for
their distinguishing characteristic is that the adults have
elected to separate from each other.   Families   that   travel
the   A   route   separate   before   appropriate action has been
taken,   those   taking   Route   B   use   separation   as   their
appropriate action.

The   third   type of modifed family is the kind in which
there is no separation or divorce but there is   a   reduction
in   personnel. This   reduction   can   come   about because of
death, hospitalization or   other   institutionalization,   or
through   normal   growing-up   processes. If   the person that
leaves or dies is a parent, the family is classified   as   C1
and it is included with separated families.[*] If one   of   the
younger   generation   leaves, the family is classified as C2.
In the latter case, the reorganization is more   like   intact
families, so C2 families are included with them.

Different   from   the   modified   families   are the intact
ones. They have the same personnel   as   before,   only   their
patterns are changed.

Regardless   of   their   route   of crisis resolution, all
families have some similar problems. In other ways, each   of
these   routes   has   unique   problems   and   advantages. These
similarities and unique features are the subject of the rest
of the chapter.

Similarities During Reorganization

There are problems that all families must   face   during
the   Period of Reorganization. The crisis process involves a
second order change and this means   that   families   need   to
rebuild   both the structure of their values and their manner
of behaving. Some do this successfully and some do not   but,
regardless   of   their   success,   they all face confusion and
anxiety. Confusion   is   cleared   through   consolidation
processes   and   anxiety   is   alleviated in rebounding. These
general problems of confusion   and   anxiety   are   our   first
focus.

The   meeting   of   needs   during   Reorganization   is   an
important matter and personal needs and family structure are
intertwined. Let us consider one need, that of being seen as
a whole person, and note the way the problem is   related   to

---

[*]   By parent, I mean the person playing a parental role. If
the   person   that   dies   is   a marginally involved grand
parent in a three generation household, the family would
be   included   in   the   C2   category. If   an   active,
responsible,   and   parental   older   son   were the one to
leave, the family would be classifed as C1.

confusion which has its source in family structural change. Being seen as a whole person is aided by one's acceptance by others. This acceptance is advanced by a general consistency in the behavior of the self and others.[4] It is this consistency that is upset by the confusion which is a part of the crisis process. The desire for consistency in one's self and in one's intimate relations promotes efforts toward image congruency. When the congruency is attained confusion and anxiety are reduced. This congruency will, in turn, promote more and general family consistency and this will promote a whole person perspective.

Families are expected to fulfill other needs. Whether the families reorganize as modified or intact, they must still see to it that members are fed and housed and clothed. In this day and age, personal growth is also a family responsibility. Families have reasons for existing and if the commitment of members is to be maintained, these reasons must be realized.

The crisis process makes the meeting of individuals' needs difficult. Families usually operate at high energy levels and there is little kept in reserve for emergencies. A crisis is just such an emergency and when extra effort is made in one part of the family system the energy is taken from activity in some other area. Needs that are usually met go begging.

Besides their needs, families during Reorganization are similar in that society maintains general expectations for them and little allowance is made for the type of organization. One parent or two, it does not matter for children are still expected to go to school and behave themselves, families are still expected to pay their bills, they are still the agency of consumption. The family cannot deal with its problems in a vacuum for other institutions make demands and these demands seldom take the family's structure, organization, or number of persons into account.

Another similarity is that the crisis process will effect different family members in discrepant ways. Family dynamics, regardless of the degree of the family's intactness, are complex and felt by family members differently. The process of negotiation of new roles and the sharing of new values requires that family members give of themselves and some must give more than others.

All families have to deal with the values and behavior that existed in the old system. During Reorganization, shadows of the former organization reassert themselves.

---

[4] Elliot Aronson, The Social Animal (San Francisco: W.H. Freeman, 1972), pp. 203-233.

98

Behavior has precedents and habit is strong. The hammering out of a new set of consistent patterns means that many established patterns have to be changed to fit with the new pattern. However important this new pattern is, the power of the old patterns is substantial and old and discarded patterns are seductive in their familiarity.

Finally, all families have gone through a difficult time. They have a sense of themselves as a family that they did not have before. For better or worse, they can not go back. Their experience has changed them both as individuals and as a group.

Special Circumstances

As the preceding has indicated, families have some similarities during Reorganization and these similarities are independent of the kind of family being reorganized. In the following, the focus will be on the advantages and disadvantages of families during Reorganization as relative advantage is related to the family's structure, personnel, and route through Reorganization.

Commonalities of modifed families and differences between them and intact families. In some ways, modified families are similar to each other and these commonalities are not shared by intact families. In the first place, modified families are non-normative. Although the rising divorce rate has produced a higher percentage of single parent families, the normal North American family is still considered to consist of a husband and a wife and their dependent children.

Non-mormality has advantages and disadvantages during Reorganization. Its disadvantages center around the pejorative context into which it is placed and this context increases the need for rebounding. The resulting difficulty in maintaining a self image which includes competence and worth is a problem that people in intact families do not face. Another disadvantage is that most people have not grown up in families in which a divorce has taken place and they have no role models to follow. The result is confusion for there is no way to learn the role except by trial and error.

On the advantage side, the non-normative family has more alternatives open to it. Not being constrained by sterotypical role behavior, the modified family can develop inter-generational coalitions, and non-sex-specific behavior in terms of its own needs and talents. There is more freedom to improvise.

Intact families, being the standard, are more locked into culturally prescribed ways of doing things. Roles are familiar to the point of being automatic, expectations are clear and consistent, and these expectations are reinforced by society, that is by other institutions, agencies, and people in general. This makes intact families more stable and less flexible than modified families.

Besides being non-normative, modified families have departed to a larger degree from the family which existed previously. Not only can they improvise more, they _must_, for there are more changes to be made. There are more new patterns to be established, more new values to be negotiated. If the families are separated ones, (Routes A,B) the input of the no-longer present parent is less strongly felt and the remaining parent can build the family more on the basis of his/her own ideals. Modified families have fewer residues of the past with which to be concerned.[5]

The third major difference between modified and intact families is that the former have fewer adults. Families, even with two adults, are as Hill put it, "badly handicapped organizationally".[6] Take away one adult and its composition is more heavily weighted with dependants, it becomes more puny as a work group, and it becomes less ideally manned to withstand stress. Intact families have the potential of being more effective during reorganization. The confusion arising from crisis is not increased by special problems arising from a new family organization. With the same adults with known abilities, the family is a more able task force.

There are special problems with which the modified family, especially the separated family, must contend. Consider the problem of socialization. Both intact and modified families are expected to inculcate society's values; socialization is sometimes complicated for the separated parent. For example, if the particular value in question is that sexual needs ought to be circumscribed by marriage, the separated parent is in a tight spot. Sexual needs do not end with separation and so the single parent must decide between two alternatives. On the one hand he can support the societal view and either forego his need gratification or hide it from the kids. On the other hand, he can meet his needs and not support the social view. No such dilemma bothers the intact family.

The previous example is one which points to a general problem. The general problem is the way in which the single parent meets their needs, those needs that are usually met in the family. I would guess that most single parents choose need fulfillment over institutional support. The logical

---

[5] This is a special problem for intact families and will be discussed in greater length below.
[6] Hill, "Generic Features of Families under Stress," p. 140.

outcome is that children see their parents' needs being met in non-family ways and this may result in the children's reduced commitment to the marriage institution as a source of need fulfillment.

The fifth special characteristic of modified families is a reduction in income or in available money. In case of separation, the wife usually gets the children and, since she is infrequently the main bread winner, she usually experiences a sharp drop in living standard.[7] The man also is usually not as well off financially for he now has two households to which to contribute. Where death has been the source of the family's modification, the financial strains are obvious and well known. In the case of the death of a young parent, the survivor must do without either the financial or the home-making services. Although there are many other losses involved, these are financially relevant.

Related to this, is the loss in social standing. Being a divorced person, being a single parent, and even being a widow or widower is to be at a lower social level than being a member of an intact family. Being married is the "proper state" of an adult in contemporary North American society and to be otherwise is somehow not quite right. Of course, this is less true of the elderly but, alas, we hardly ever think of them anyway.

Quite frequently, social assistance is made available to single parents. This may help them over the financial difficulties but it does little for their feelings of self worth. The reduction of personal rights and the attack on pride that usually accompanies the "bestowal" of public monies is a clear indication to the newly indigent that there has been a reduction in status. One final point is that women who received their status from their husband's position will be deprived of this reflected glory. The loss will be virtually total in separation and partial in death. That may be a very bitter pill indeed.

Another difference between modified and intact families is that modified families make more changes in their lives. In a separation, someone has to leave the family home and finding a new place is frequently difficult and always unsettling. Finding a new place to live or moving to a new community to start anew are tactics of the modified family. It may be therapeutic to make these changes but it takes energy of which the family may have precious little to spare. The intact family generally stays put.

---

[7] Ruth A. Brandwein, C.A. Brown, and E.M. Fox, "Women and Children Last: The Social Situation of Divorced Women and Their Families," Journal of Marriage and the Family, 36, 1974, pp. 498-514.

A problem of people in modified families is the re-emergence of old personal difficulties. Sometimes, people get married because of personal needs and problems that they cannot solve themselves. Sometimes the problem's impact is blunted by marriage. With the return to the non-married state, the former difficulty may reassert itself. Moreover, the reappearance of the problem is complicated by children, new personal problems such as those associated with bereavement or separation, and by an inability to remember former coping methods. Intact families do not have this particular difficulty for the relationship entered into as a solution to personal difficulties continues to cover personal limitations.

Finally, the modified family frequently sees its status as temporary. The separated and widowed know that others in these categories remarry and so a precedent is set. Moreover the special difficulties just mentioned encourage remarriage. Reorganization is made more difficult by the possibility of another relationship because two kinds of planning are necessitated. The first kind covers the immediate situation and a second kind covers the eventuality of another change. It is difficult enough to establish one set of plans; it is doubly difficult to get reorganized if these plans are considered to be provisional and subject to a future major change. On the other side, the intact family is strengthened by its satisfactory progress through crisis and this new strength reinforces its permanence.

In summary, the tasks of modified families are facilitated because they are more free in establishing structure, there are more alternatives from which to choose, they are not so influenced by the former system, and there are fewer adults whose desires must be accommodated. Modified families are hindered by their non-normative label, by their more limited scope as a task group, by their inability to meet the needs of family members, by their lowered social and economic status, by their having more drastic changes to make and by the future's uncertainty.

Although I will qualify this later, intact families seem to have numerically fewer problems during Reorganization. Their income, status, organization, geographic location are more stable. They are normative and internal processes are supported by society. They should feel more confident of themselves and more sure of their ability to handle forthcoming problems. They are more able to make definite plans for the future and work to see them come to flower.

Differences among modified families. The existence of types of modified families implies differences between the types. The focus will be on the differences between separated families, those taking Routes A and B, and developmentally reorganized families, those taking Route C1.

One special part of the lives of separated people is their dealing with their former spouse. It is clear that when loving relations turn sour the result is sometimes characterized by bitterness. The divorce process as it generally works in North America can only be said to intensify these feelings. Strong feelings of hate, just as strong love feelings, make free choice among alternatives very difficult. With love, a person takes into considerations the desires of the loved one and chooses that which will promote other's joy. With hate, the person takes into consideration the desires of the hated person and chooses so as to hurt that person. In neither situation does the person choose in terms of his own feelings and best interests. What may be necessary is a feeling of neutral affect. This neutrality is difficult to obtain because the past is still hurtful and because the relationship may still involve difficult interaction problems such as those related to parenting. The period of Reorganization is difficult if one's former spousal relationship intrudes.

It would be incorrect to assume that all relationships among the separated are uniform. Separated couples differ in the degree that they like each other and in the amount and the ways that they interact. Relationships differ to the degree that their affect and interaction levels provide for the growth and well-being of those involved. One couple may find that they can grow more as individuals and as parents if they separate and continue to helpfully interact. They can continue to be wise parents and plan and work together for the benefit of all parties. At the other end would be found the couples who dislike each other intensely, this dislike leading to heavy expenditures of time and energy. For them, growth and well-being are of secondary importance.

In between these two family types are variations in affect and involvement. These two dimensions are idiosyncratically combined to reflect the personalities and needs of those just separated. Two such formerly married people may find growth and well-being to be advanced by the limitation of interaction because of its hostility. Two others may find extensive interaction in mutual support to be growth enhancing. Still another couple may find the relationship to be convivial but perceive growth to be advanced by keeping the interaction limited. It is doubtful that high negative affect would ever be combined with close involvement in a growth-promoting situation. This would seem to be a logical possibility only.

Re-establishing the former relationship in terms of growth possibilities is a problem that does not exist for other modified families in the same way. Where there is a death, the dead spouse is not interacted with in the same way as a separated spouse. There is not the feeling of hostility and although memory may be strong and the deceased spouse's presence felt as though he were still alive, this feeling dissipates over time and the person becomes more free of the other's influence. In cases of a family member's institutionalization, usually the amount of interaction is limited and specifically controlled. With the limitation on interaction, the spouse at home is free to deal with matters the way they wish.

The second special situation of separated families is that they have been through the divorce process. Families that have gone through legal proceedings associated with separation and divorce have had to do all or some of the following things. They have had to prove their unworthiness or that of their spouse. They have had to lie, feel guilty, feel hostile toward a former loved one, air their family secrets publically, demand from or bestow support upon someone from whom they want total independence. They deal with lawyers who are primarily in it for the money and there are fights over property. Finally, they have to deal with their children and, worst of all, the children can be drawn into the fray as tokens in the settlement hassle. The divorce process rubs quite raw the sores already opened by this difficult personal life change. The divorce process, in effect, punishes those who are unwilling to any longer stay in a bad marriage. This punishment affects their views of themselves, their children, marriage in general, and other cross-sex people.

During separation and divorce, the legal system intrudes into the family area. The adversary approach, with its requirement of individual wrong doing and its need to fix responsibility, is detrimental to quality relationships. The legal system applies its standards to a situation which was not organized to comply with legalities. Guilt and blame and grounds and me-against-you and bargaining and condonation and the very idea that a judge can refuse to grant a divorce are all interjected into the couple's relationship. The couple's interaction is changed for all time and future possibilities for effective dealings are rendered difficult.

In order to get the best settlement, others' values and standards and strategies are employed. The result is that the relationship becomes a means and not an end in itself. The other person with whom interaction must still take place becomes a dark stranger. The separated person has a big task and this is to move away from the confusion created by the split and the destructive attacks that are a part of the legal divorce. This movement is needed in order to get a clear view of the present situation and future needs and possibilities. This clarity is aided by a strong sense of self, a certainty that one has acted in terms of their own feelings and standards, and a strong conviction that quality relationships are possible.

People in families being modified because of

development are usually better able to clearly see their
individual worth and their future alternatives for they have
not had guilt and failure pushed upon them. A lowered self
image is more likely to be found among divorced and
separated people than among widows and widowers. A
separation can be related to either poor choosing or poor
maintenance and failure in either instance points to
incompetence. People rarely feel guilty for either the death
or the institutionalization of a loved one so image
restructuring is less of a problem.

Another source of variation is found in the view of
marriage held by those who are separated and those whose
spouse has died. It is likely that separated people would
view marriage as more problematic than would the others. The
marriage survivor, on the other hand, may feel cheated and
bitter but it is unlikely that the bitterness would be seen
as arising from the marriage institution.

Families whose Reorganization is necessitated by death
have advantages over separated families in that the event is
fixed in time, bereavement is institutionalized, closure
takes place and life can again be taken up. All this takes
place in a short period of time rather than the way it is in
separation and divorce in which years may pass before the
Reorganization can begin. The swiftness of death can be seen
as problematic in the short run because it is too direct and
unsettling. In the long run, however, I believe there are
advantages to a sharp and clear break. Some of the benefits
are a minimum of residues from the past, a jolt which
clearly indicates the necessity of reorganization, and the
removal of the former spouse from the scene so that
reorganization can be more directly aimed at those
immediately involved.

Differences among separated families. Families that
come to dissolution by Route A with an exit prior to
appropriate action are different from those families which
come to dissolution as a result of appropriate action. The
Route A families, not being able to correct their problem
situation, are dealing from a position of weakness. They are
likely to be confused about what has happened and they will
perceive incompetence in themselves. It is quite possible
that they are incompetent and unable to deal successfully
with other people. If this incompetence has its source in
family dynamics, they may have more success during
Reorganization than they had before. If the incompetence is
a reflection of deep-set personality problems,
Reorganization will be as filled with failure as were former
parts of the crisis process.

Route B families, those coming to dissolution as an
appropriate solution, have acted in a definite and
purposeful manner. They have convinced themselves that they
know what has gone wrong and what they must do to resolve

the problem. This should encourage both a sense of competence and the competence itself. Both of these aspects of success are of crucial importance during Reorganization where feeling competent and actually being competent are vital to correct decision making and appropriate implementation.

The special situation of intact families. Intact families do not have many of the problems of the modified families. They have no great reduction in income or increase in expenses, they have feelings of accomplishment, a heightened sense of family unity, a known set of available talents, and a stable task group. The one disadvantage that intact families have, and it is a substantial one, is that the residues of the former structure are omnipresent. We have seen that one of the major tasks during Reorganization is to consolidate the new pattern by fitting it congruently with other family behavior. This is definitely more difficult for intact families for there are remnants of the old patterns that are constant reminders of the way things used to be. Their problem is to change many of their older patterns to be congruent with the singular new one and this is difficult because there will be a general tendency to revert to the comfortable patterns that existed in the past.

Modified families have no such problem. Theirs has been a dramatic change that has reverberated clearly throughout the family system and this change has struck down some former patterns and changed most others. As noted before, modified families have numerically greater problems but the solving of them is simplified because the past is not so likely to intrude.

Although consolidation is in some ways easier for modified families, rebounding is easier for intact families. Because intact families have an established group with high levels of consensus, established methods of operation, high levels of security, and a definition of themselves as permanent, they present a unit with the requisites for rebounding success. They should be well able to allay anxiety for they see their continued unity as an important and on-going quality and they are well equipped to again move into the future with harmony.

FAMILY STRENGTHS

A family's success in consolidating and rebounding is related to:

1.   Its ability to make its patterns consistent. This depends on:

A.   The amount of value-behavior consistency.
B.   Image congruency.

106

C. Its ability to handle residues from former interation.

2. Its success during Secondary Adjustment.

3. Its ability to use outside assistance or ignore damaging intrusions.

4. The extent to which personal needs are being met.

5. The speed at which reorganization takes place.

6. The extent to which it sees its situation as permanent.

7. Its freedom to choose from among a number of alternatives.

8. The existence of institutionalized patterns which fit the family's needs.

This completes the model. We have traced the activities of families through the entire crisis process: we have seen them work their way into difficulty, deal with the stressor, and then rebuild their personal lives and their family's life around the required new values and behavior.

CHAPTER 6

LOOKING BACKWARD AND FORWARD

I have been advised that this chapter should be brief,
that readers in general, and students specifically, dislike
chapters that prolong a book past some reasonable stopping
point. With that in mind, this chapter will be only long
enough to satisfy the need for closure. To round out the
inquiry, I will summarize what I have learned or had
reaffirmed about families in crisis, especially noting the
characteristics of ably functioning families. In the last
part of the chapter, I will consider the model's use as a
therapeutic tool and with that we will bring closure to this
inquiry.

FAMILY DYNAMICS AND CRISIS

Since all families at one time or another face crisis,
their dynamics, that is, their interaction processes, their
changing structure, and their personnel variation, have been
a major concern in this inquiry. The result is that the
consideration of crisis specifically has led to an increased
understanding of general family dynamics I have learned
some things about families and the importance of other
elements has been reaffirmed. These ideas I will share with
you for your consideration and evaluation. You might well
select different insights as being more important; the
following, however, are the ones I wish to emphasize.

Value Congruency

The ideas of family members merge into the family mind,
the shared way that family members view the world. David
Cooper[1] has pointed out that the family mind is damaging
because youngsters must accept this mind and they discount
their own experience when it contradicts that which others
hold to be true. Although I believe his observation to be
valid, and something which every parent should very
carefully consider, there seems to be no way to establish a
family without such closeness in thinking. Moreover, this
inquiry has indicated that congruent thinking is
instrumental in encouraging crisis resolution.

The instrumentality of congruent thinking arises from
its ability to free families from negotiating their values.
Thus freed, they can directly expend their energies on

---

[1]   Cooper, David. The Death of the Family (Harmondsworth:
Penguin, 1972).

making their patterns consistent with their goals and other basic values. Without basic value consistency, negotiation of the direction to take must occur before any movement happens.

It is usually not the content of the family mind that leads to crisis, it is usually an inability to implement values because of incongruency somewhere in the system. A family that agrees on the proper (proper for them, that is) balance of separateness and connectedness, the way that husband-wife and other important roles should be played, the importance of unity and personal growth, is usually successful. Agreement leads to success as families can concentrate on ways to implement their consensus.

Incongruity delays concerted action as compromise must precede activity and compromise at basic value levels is problematic. Compromise of lower level values and behavior consists of matching means to ends and is the stuff with which group life is perpetually involved. However, the compromise of basic level values is hazardous. If the deep values are surrendered, the person giving in will feel a loss in either their personal integrity or power or both. A reaction is likely. If behavior changes without deep values being touched, the behavior change will be temporary despite the best intentions and strongest expectations for the deep values will eventually reassert themselves.

Basic level incongruity can be reduced by finding and appealing to some still more basic level value. The quid pro quo[2] therapeutic technique of something for something, this for that, in which each person gives up something of equal value is based on the idea that unity is the ultimate value and more important than that which is being surrendered. Incongruity can also be reduced if one person can be led to see the internal inconsistencies among his basic values and he chooses to change to reduce the personal inconsistency and thereby increase wider system congruency.

Basic level congruency is advantageous. Congruency increases the liklihood of obtaining the priceless unessentials. Spontaneity and predictability grow out of basic level agreement and life is satisfying when behavior is sincere and genuine and when it occurs with acceptance and without the thought of consequences. The relationship in which this occurs becomes highly valued.

With basic level congruence, a person's integrity is not questioned for his behavior makes sense to other family members. No explanations are necessary because the others simply understand. With congruence there is the liklihood

---

[2] Lederer and Jackson, op. cit.

that all family members will be seen as whole persons, the
ultimate pay-off of family life, and that their feelings,
knowledge, and experience will be accepted and valued. With
this acceptance comes a commitment to the family and the
concomitant willingness to keep the family together and ably
functioning.

Value/Behavior Agreement

Another important family element is the degree of
agreement between values and behavior. It is strange to
think that a family would organize its behavior so as to
subvert its values but this is sometimes the case. The
subversion may arise from ignorance or the wish for personal
gain. It may be that the family members do not see the
explicit consequences or the subtle implications of their
behavior. It may be that they are directed to take a short-
run view which is counter to their long term goals. It may
be that personal needs become momentarily elevated and
family goals and values are lowered. At any rate, there are
times when behavior is not synchronized with values and this
usually means inappropriateness in execution or correction
patterns and, as we have seen, such inappropriateness is an
initial step in family crisis.

Execution patterns are quite mundane and uninteresting
as long as they are working well. Correction patterns are
more interesting and vital to the family's value/behavior
consistency. Correction patterns carry the family's burden
of flexibility. If nothing else, I have tried to indicate
that a family's health depends on its being able to
creatively anticipate and intelligently adjust to changes in
itself and in its environment. This flexibility is essential
but it is a flexibility that must be grounded in the
family's values as these give flexibility a meaning.

Families that have the greatest success in crisis
usually perceive change to be imminent and consider all
their states to be temporary. They highly value their family
experience and wish it to continue. There is an openness for
each person's feelings and knowledge and experience and this
openness is associated with mutual acceptance. In short,
information which might be useful is readily exchanged and
treated as important. Thus armed, these happy and ably
functioning families can correct their inappropriateness so
that the family not only functions, but its functioning
furthers the basic values and goals of each member and all
members.

Sound Structure

Families that function well have sound structures with
distinct yet reasonable divisions. The most important
division, and one which has been considered earlier, is the
generational one. Generational coalitions allow the

111

youngster to develop his own patterns of response to the world. The child can grow without adult pressures and responsibilities bothering his age-specific needs. The coalition gives parents space to be objective and to be directive when direction is appropriate. The space also requires that parents work out their spousal problems with each other, without involving the child as a tension release. It is most important that the family's structure be such that the child be taken into the family, accepted as a valued part, and then be provided with the opportunity to become a separate person and to leave the family when the time comes.

Special Characteristics

The last of the categories contains a collection of special characteristics which families find useful during crisis. Families that work well usually have the ability to take risks. Either someone in the family moves the family to attempt new ways or to consider new ideas or the family as a whole is innovative and has an experimental mien. Total family congruency is not helpful at this point for with perfect congruency there is insufficient mix to generate alternatives. Risk taking and innovation are especially important during the Secondary Adjustment Period when the solution to the problem is being considered and when appropriate action is formulated.

The family is well off that can function as an efficient problem solving group. If family members have the ability to clearly and accurately perceive the problem's extent, its source, and the level at which remedial activity can take place, it will quickly emerge from the crisis if it acts harmoniously on the knowledge.

Finally, families that work well do not get bogged down in meaningless conflict. When conflict emerges it is allowed to escalate, basic values are considered, and the matter is resolved as appropriate. The conflict-related issue can then be approached; the issue may be the conflict's explicit content, it may be some family rule, or the conflict may be merely a way of reducing tension. Whatever the problem, understanding is increased and resolution occurs. Families which function best deal only once with a particular conflict for resolution occurs before the issue is put away. By so doing, the family does not fall victim to negative feedback loops and these loop's ability to dissipate the corrective force of contentious issues.

These are some of the characteristics of ably functioning families that help them through the crisis process. We now move to the consideration of the therapeutic implications of the model.

THE MODEL'S USE IN THERAPY

This section will consist of three parts. The initial
part will concern the model's general insights that I
believe are helpful to family therapists. The second and
third sections are more specific; the second section
explains the model's use in diagnosing family difficulties
and the third considers the model's use in intervention.

General Insights

The model helps most generally to sensitize the
therapist to certain family dynamics which are crucial to
its continued viability. Most therapists look for particular
patterns which they have seen detrimentally operating in
families. They then intervene on the basis of their
perception and some formula which has worked previously.
Their success starts with the clarity of their perception
and the skill with which they get the family to correct
their inappropriate patterns. The model can help therapists
to isolate the family's problem, it can help in the
development of a therapeutic program, it may even point to
some broad intervention strategies. It cannot, however,
specify intervention as these must be particular to the
families and to the therapists skill and approach.

The general insights which will be discussed are
extensions of the model's two theoretical bases, the
developmental theory and the systems approach. The model
produces a particular therapeutic orientation which is
expressed in certain goals and procedures. We will first
discuss the orientation and then the procedural issues.

Orientation. The orientation of the theory, the model,
and the associated therapy is decidedly interactional. The
emphasis is on the group rather than the individual. Cause
and effect thinking are minimized and each part's
relationship to the whole and to every other part is
emphasized.

The ideas expressed in the previous paragraph clearly
indicate that the family rather than the individual is the
object of treatment. While the group orientation is crucial,
the individual is a vital element and maintaining proper
balance between a family orientation and an individualistic
perspective is essential if therapy is to be successful.
Families are precious but individuals are equally so and the
therapy that works best promotes health at both levels.

Keeping system levels separate is essential to analysis
for only in this way can the family's effect on the
individual be seen and the members' effect on family
functioning be determined. The separation of systems allows
the therapist to change the family system by changing a
member and the therapist can affect an individual's behavior

113

through a revision of the family's interaction patterns.

The time orientation is decidedly present tense. The future is seen as being less important than the present and increasingly less important as it becomes more remote. The past is hardly important at all. Although the present builds on the past, the past cannot be changed and whether or not it can even be understood, given the lack of objectivity, the failing of memory, and the defensive behavior associated with its discussion, is questionable. The present, however, can be observed, troubles diagnosed, and interventions made. This is sociology not history.

Another orientation element is a focus on the family's unique situation. No two families are alike and successful therapy must be based on the existence of differences. The model would be mishandled if it were used to either see families in crisis as being identical or if it considered their movement through the crisis process to be programmed by the process. There are family similarities to be sure and the model suggests probable common steps. There is, however, no assurance that all families or any family will perfectly fit the model. There are many family organizational structures, many kinds of interaction patterns, many kinds of stressors, and the needs of families and their members differ significantly. The therapist must find out the family's uniqueness and figure ways to make the most of their special talents while minimizing the impact of their failings.

That a family is unique is true and it is equally certain that it shares some of its characteristics with other families. I believe that families ought to be made aware of their similarities with and differences between themselves and other families. The therapist knows these things and uses the similarities and differences to help families. The sharing of the therapist's perception suggests the acceptance of the differences and similarities. The acceptance of the family as it is, that is, the acceptance of its point in a process leading to health, is the first step in moving toward change.

The major goal of therapy is to enable families to solve their problems. Since the family spends most of its time away from direct contact with the therapist and since it must handle a number of different issues which are not topics during therapeutic sessions, the job of the therapist must be to help the family to strengthen itself so that it can act appropriately. The family's inappropriateness must be stopped and new patterns established and attendant problems solved. The therapist can use many techniques to break destructive patterns and these techniques can include paradoxical intervention, directive or non-directive activity and instructional intervention. These techniques must be tailor made to the family's problems and the

114

therapists expertise. They will all work with the model as a
basis and they all can be used to help the family change
themselves.

Procedural issues. The model indicates that
dysfunctional negative feedback loops are at the root of the
problem for they have allowed inappropriateness to continue
and to be strengthened through the accommodation of other
patterns. One of the therapeutic requirements is to somehow
prevent the family's use of negative feedback loops; the
therapist must facilitate a switch to positive loops. This
will likely be difficult as the family has rules against
such risky, confrontational, and, frequently, conflict
ridden patterns. The therapist's task is to initiate such
activities and stand ready to insure that the family
resolves the issue, learns ways to resolve similar issues,
and completes the episode by successfully dealing with
tangential matters. The therapist must see that the family
stays on topic; he must provide integration when
disintegration is rampant. Most important, he must lead the
family to the understanding that positive feedback loops are
essential to long-term adequate family functioning and that
they can occur without being disastrous in the short-term.

Another procedural issue concerns the family's
receptivity to change during the disorganization following a
stressor. The wallowing and confusion that is a part of
disorganization contains the seeds of new patterns as well
as the remains of the old. Families are sometimes receptive
to being helped to bring their scattered remnants together
in ways which will enable them to accomplish their goals.
Having failed to handle well a predictable stressor or to
deal successfully with an unpredictable one, they have
experienced pain and the likelihood is that they would like
to be able to accomplish their ends in a more agreeable
manner.

Another therapeutic issue is the family's values.
Therapy has a higher chance for success if the therapist can
see the source of difficulty. This perception helps him to
make appropriate intervention. Putting aside his or her own
values, the therapist must consider if the family's values
are consistent or inconsistent, if there is agreement
between the strong family members, if values are such that
disorganization-from-paranoia or disorganization-from-
naivite results, or if the family has difficulty because of
an inability to express their appropriate values with
consistent and effective behavior patterns.

The model has suggested that speed in therapy is
essential. This fits with the brief therapy idea suggesting
that short-term therapy has advantages over long-term
therapy. The advantages accrue from the reduction in
tangential problems. In this context, the delay of therapy
while histories are taken or while all of the relevant facts

are gathered is seen as harmful. A family that has indicated
its willingness to correct itself deserves immediate help
and that can begin in the earliest stages of therapy.

And finally, the model gives direction to therapy. It
helps the therapist make analysis of specific elements which
may be dysfunctional. The complexity of families leads to
confusion and without specifics to look for the therapist is
likely to be lost. With the model, the therapist can look
for the source of the problem in a number of places and deal
specifically with the inappropriate bits of family life. He
is also encouraged to see these bits as fitting into the
wider family system and he should be able to better see
their wider ramifications.

Using the Model to Diagnose

The therapist has two tasks. The first is to figure out
what is wrong and the second is to do something about it. In
this section the concern is to explain how the model can
help the therapist determine what is amiss.

Generally, the therapist must ask himself "What is
going on here?" Out of the confusion the therapist must be
able to draw some sensible conclusions. He must ascertain
why the family acts the way it does and what purpose, if
any, the crisis serves for the family. The model will help
him analyze the situation.

The therapist must get through the confusion to the
real issues. The family is likely to be disorganized and
their perceptions of what is wrong differ. After all, if
they had some agreed-upon appropriate solution they would
not need therapy. But they disagree and there is the
likelihood that each family member wants the therapist to
accept his definition of the problem. Of course, the
therapist must resist these attempts at entanglement and
remain free to make alignments and otherwise get involved so
as to accomplish change. But, prior to the intervention
comes the diagnosis and having a framework helps the
therapist withstand both the family's attempt and family
members' attempts to seduce him (the therapist) into the
family's pattern of inappropriateness.

The therapist must determine whether the source of the
problem is in the family's transactions, its intramural
activities, or in the behavior of a family member. The
system's view sees these levels as being intertwined and
indeed they are. Nevertheless, analysis requires that they
be separated and independently investigated. Somewhere the
monstrous and apparently monolithic family system must be
broken into and disturbed. The disturbance should be at the
place where the therapist has found the inappropriateness to
be located and where it can be corrected. The model's
emphasis on the interdependence of systems levels and the

116

need for their separate analysis should help the therapist successfully break into and enter the family.

The model provides the therapist with a framework against which the family can be placed for analysis. Of course, the family's patterns are real in a sense that the model can never be. However, the model suggests some issues, problematic patterns, and action requirements that may apply to a family at a particular time. The validity to a particular family of the hunches that the model provides can be found and if the hunches are correct the therapist will have an idea of the family's place in the crisis process and what he must do to be of assistance.

I indicated in the previous section that the model's orientation was such that negative feedback loops were seen as important. In most instances, the diagnosis of the family's difficulties is the diagnosis of their negative feedback loops. If the stressor is predictable, the diagnosis would focus on the negative loops which prevented correction before the stressor. These loops need somehow to be changed so that they do not operate in the same way in the future. In fact, the therapist will not be successful in helping the family until he upsets these patterns for they will exist to subvert the therapist's best plans and most innovative interventions.

If the crisis is related to an unpredictable stressor, the therapist will be led by the model to consider why the family's efforts fail, that is, why the family makes unsatisfactory progress through secondary adjustment. The model can be particularly helpful for the steps which families normally take are indicated and the therapist can determine at what point the family is having difficulty.

Therapy does not only deal with inadequacies, it also deals with family strengths. Therapy will fail unless the family's strong points can be incorporated into it. The model assists the therapist in determining family strengths. The therapist can see if strength lies in the execution or correction patterns, in neither or in both. The model can sensitize the therapist to the existence of a sponsor who will precipitate change. The model has dealt extensively with values and could be used to determine the family's strengths in its value consistency and its ability to effectively match behavior with values. These are important strengths and ones which can be built upon.

The model can be used in diagnosis to determine whether the family's problem is chronic or transitory. A chronic problem would be indicated by inadequacy in correction patterns, strong negative feedback loops, problems with predictable stressors, the failure of family members to take responsibility, value incongruency, and disharmony between values and behavior. These are a few of the indications of

117

chronicity which the model presents and these are elements which the therapist can look for. Acute problems are indicated by an unpredictable stressor's falling upon a family which had been functioning successfully. These families need support and their effective patterns warrant reinforcement. Since the treatment of momentarily upset families is so different from the treatment of the chronically dysfunctional ones, the diagnosis which differentiates between the two is crucial. The model helps the therapist to differentiate.

Intervention

The therapist has now diagnosed the problem and she and the family now must do something about it. I believe the model can be helpful at this therapeutic stage.

The model can be very helpful for therapists who educate their clients. One way of bringing order out of chaos is for the family members to understand their location in the crisis process and know what remains to accomplish. The graphic representation can be used to indicate to the family the "YOU ARE HERE" point and if they see their tasks as a series of one-at-a-time steps the future may seem less ominous. The family's acceptance that at least someone, the therapist, knows what is happening and that others have passed this way before will likely have an uplifting effect. The family's disorder will be more likely seen as temporary if it is placed in a context of a passing and important stage of development.

The model can be useful in therapy aimed at helping families avoid stressors. Again, using an instructional approach, families can be shown the importance of execution and correction patterns. They can be helped to more accurately judge when these are working satisfactorily. The early determination of execution pattern inefficiency is important to family functioning. With ample time, correction patterns can be employed and shortcomings in all paterns can be corrected.

In addition, crisis prevention as suggested by the model, would have families appraised of the importance of handling information exchange so that the family is open enough to admit helpful information and closed enough to deal with this information in a family-supportive way. Prevention would also touch upon value agreement and the importance of each person's ideas, experience, and perception. If basic values are inconsistent, an agreement to disagree will likely be helpful. This agreement is based on an appeal to some more basic value (whether it be family unity, personal growth, elan vital, or whatever) so that the disagreement is seen as less important than the support of the still-more-basic value.

The use of the model can be used to help the therapist generate functional positive feedback loops. When the therapist attempts to help the family move toward more satisfying patterns, the family will attempt to block her interventions. The model suggests some ways that the therapist can circumvent the family's efforts. The therapist can unbalance the family system. The family attempts to remain stable and uses negative feedback loops to keep it on an even, albeit dysfunctional, level. The therapist can unbalance the system by supporting some particular member and continuing to support him in the face of family pressure to the contrary. The support will unbalance the system and then, if attempts to re-establish the status quo are prevented, the family's rules or methods will necessarily change.

The therapist runs the risk, of course, of alienating herself and the supported family member from the rest of the family unless some adequate and careful preparatory work has been accomplished. The therapist must not side with just the one person but find elements of ideas from others that warrant support. The therapist might also announce that she will support one person and then another depending upon what she felt was best for the system. These approaches minimize a person's being left out with rebellion remaining as the only way to save face. The best defense against alienation is the family's understanding that the therapist is sincere and knowledgeable and that she is supportive of them as individuals and as parts of a family.

In a similar way, the therapist can work with the family member who is most eager to correct the system. It is unlikely that this person will be the most powerful member (if the sponsor were most powerful, the family would probably not be in therapy) and so the support must be handled with care so that the power shift is acceptable. Again, however, such support will unbalance the system and initiate a positive feedback loop. The therapist must then keep the escalation going until deep values are reached, provide integration for the family while it works through the value differences, supervise the family's efforts to bring closure, and then help them to deal with the new rule, the changed relationship, and the better chances for family strength and individual growth.

Another way to launch a positive feedback loop is to prevent a family member from "sacrificing themselves for the good of the family". Of course, such sacrifice is superficial and the martyr gets their unjust desserts in sympathy, other's guilt, and forbearance while the family remains a mess. The therapist needs to block these efforts and can do so in a number of ways. One way is to make them explicit, not by pointing out their damaging effects, but by indicating them to be "for the protection" of the other family members and mentioning their high cost to the martyr.

Or, the therapist can point out the benefits for all family members when one member bears the brunt. In this way the homeostatic device will be rendered impotent and the regenerative activity of the positive feedback loop can have a chance.

The destruction of the family's negative feedback loop mechanisms is an essential element of therapy based on this model. I have attempted to show that it is as risky and complicated as it is essential.

In the family that has recently experienced the stressor, the model can help guide intervention strategies. In the first place, the impact of the stressor must be carefully handled. The model has indicated that the family's ability to make a creative response depends in part upon the stressor's effect. If the stressor has had insufficient impact and a variable effect on family members, corrective behavior will be unlikely and the family will return to await a repeated stressor. Rather than this loss of time and gain of pain, the therapist can here emphasize how terrible the situation is and that the more they think about it the worse it will be seen to be. In addition, the weight of the stressor and the dysfunction it represents must be passed around so that each family member shares in the discomfort. Simply put, correction will not take place unless the situation is put in a very bad light and unless all family members have a stake in its correction.

On the other hand, if the stressor has had such a great impact that the family has become incapacitated, an opposite approach would be used. The therapist might well accept the disorganization as being reasonable "given the family's understanding of the situation but didn't they see ....." and then the therapist could reframe their situation and put it into a category of challenging experiences, or opportunity for family reconstruction, or what many other families have gone through and emerged better for it, or whatever the family needs to gather strength to work toward solution.

This partial listing of therapeutic applications is intended to indicate some of the ways that the model can be used. The wisdom, expertise, and training of therapists will allow them to incorporate the model in the ways which best fit their approach and methods. I leave that exercise to them.

With the completion of this section there is the completion of the chapter and the book. I have no big summary, no climax with flashing lights and fireworks, no finale. Just the hope and belief in two things. One, that I have taken a step forward in the attempt to find out about families and how they work. And two, that people in families and who work to help them now have a better means of creating family life that is intimate, continuous, and growth enhancing.

BIBLIOGRAPHY

Adams, Bert. The Family: A Sociological Interpretation. Chicago: Rand McNally, 1976.

Aldous, Joan. "The Family Developmental Approach to Family Analysis." Minneapolis, Minnesota: Department of Sociology, 1967.

Aronson, Elliot. The Social Animal. San Francisco: W.H. Freeman, 1972.

Bateson, Gregory. Steps Toward an Ecology of Mind. New York: Ballantine Books, 1972.

Black, K. Dean. "Systems Theory and the Development of the Marital Relationship," Paper presented at the Annual Meeting of the American Sociological Association, New Orleans, La, 1972.

Brandwein, Ruth A.; Brown, C.A.; and Fox, E.M. "Women and Children Last: The Social Situation of Divorced Women and Their Families," Journal of Marriage and the Family, 36 (1974), 498-514.

Burgess, Ernest W.; Lock, Harvey J.; and Thomes, Mary Margaret. The Family. New York: Van Nostrand, 1971.

Burr, Wesley R. "Satisfaction with Various Aspects of Marriage Over the Life Cycle: A Random Middle Class Sample," Journal of Marriage and the Family, 26 (1970), 29-37.

_____. "Role Transitions: A Reformulation of the Theory," Journal of Marriage and the Family, 34 (1972), 407-416.

_____. Theory Construction and the Sociology of the Family. New York: Wiley, 1973.

Cannon, Walter B. The Wisdom of the Body. New York: Norton, 1932.

Cooper, David. The Death of the Family. Harmondsworth: Penguin, 1972.

Cuber, John C. and Harroff, Peggy B. Sex and the Significant Americans. Baltimore: Penguin Books, 1965.

Duvall, Evelyn M. Family Development. New York: J.B. Lippincott Co., 1957.

Farber, Bernard. Family: Organization and Transaction. San Francisco: Chandler, 1964.

123

Gibb, Jack R. "Defensive Communication," Journal of Communication, 11 (1961), 141-148.

Glasser, Paul H. and Glasser, Lois N. Families in Crisis. New York: Harper & Row, 1970.

Greenberg, G.S. "The Family Interactional Perspective: A Study and Examination of the Work of Don D. Jackson," Family Process, 16 (December, 1977), 385-412.

Grotjahn, Martin. Psychoanalysis and the Family Neurosis. New York: Norton, 1960.

Haley, Jay. Strategies of Psychotherapy. New York: Grunes & Stratton, 1963.

Hansen, Donald and Hill, Ruben. "Families Under Stress," Handbook of Marriage and the Family, edited by Harold Christensen. Chicago: Rand McNally & Co., 1964, 782-819.

Henry, Jules. Pathways to Madness. New York: Vintage, 1965.

Hess, Robert D. and Handel, Gerald. "The Family as a Psychosocial Organization," The Psychosocial Interior of the Family, edited by Gerald Handel. Chicago: Aldine, 1967.

Hill, Reuben. Families Under Stress: Adjustment to the Crises of War, Separation and Reunion. New York: Harper, 1949.

_____. "Generic Features of Families Under Stress," Social Casework, 39 (1958), 139-150.

_____. "Modern Systems Theory and the Family: A Confrontation," Family Sociology, (1971), 264-283.

_____ and Hansen, Donald. "The Identification of Conceptual Frameworks Utilized in Family Study," Marriage and Family Living, 22 (1960), 200-311.

_____ and Rodgers, Roy H. "The Developmental Approach," Handbook in Marriage and the Family, edited by Harold Christensen, Chicago: Rand McNally & Co., 1964, 171-211.

Jackson, Don D. (ed.) Communication, Family, and Marriage. Palo Alto, CA.: Science and Behavior Books, 1968.

_____ and Lederer, William J. Mirages of Marriage. New York: Norton, 1969.

Jackson, Joan K. "The Adjustment of the Family to Alcoholism," Marriage and Family Living, 18 (1956), 361-369.

Koestler, Arthur. The Invisible Writing. New York: The Macmillan Company, 1954.

_____. The Ghost in the Machine. London: Pan Books, 1967.

Laing, R.D. The Politics of the Family and Other Essays. New York: Vintage, 1972.

_____ and Esterson, A. Sanity, Madness and the Family. Hammondsworth, Middlesex, England: Penguin, 1964.

LeMasters, Ersel E. "Parenthood as Crisis," Marriage and Family Living, 19 (1957), 352-355.

Lidz, Theodore. "The Effects of Children on Marriage," The Marriage Relationship, edited by S. Roenbaum and I. Alger. New York: Basic Books, 1968.

Lipman-Blumen, Jean. "A Crisis Framework Applied to Macrosociological Family Changes: Marriage Divorce, and Occupational trends Associated with World War II," Journal of Marriage and the Family, 37 (1975), 889-902.

Magrabi, Francis and Marshall, W.J. "Family Developmental Tasks. A Research Model," Journal of Marriage and the Family, 27 (1965), 454-461.

McCubbin, Hamilton J., Joy, Constance B., Cauble, A. Elizabeth, Comeau, Joan K., Patterson, Joam M. and Needle Richard H. "Family Stress and Coping: A Decade Review," Journal of Marriage and the Family, 42 (1980), 855-871.

Minuchin, Salvador. Families and Family Therapy. Cambridge: Harvard University Press, 1974.

Nye, F. Ivan and Berardo, Felix M. Conceptual Frameworks for the Study of the Family. New York: Macmillan Company, 1966.

Rapoport, Rhona. "Normal Crises, Family Structure and Mental Health," Family Process, 2 (1963), 68-80.

Rodgers, Roy. "Toward a Theory of Family Development," Journal of Marriage and the Family, 26 (1964), 262-270.

_____. Family Interaction and Transaction: The Developmental Approach. Englewood Cliffs, N.J.: Prentice Hall, 1973.

Rollins, Boyd C. and Bahr, Stephen. "A Theory of Power Relationships in Marriage," Journal of Marriage and the Family, 38 (1976), 619-627.

Rossi, Alice. "Transition to Parenthood," Journal of Marriage and the Family, 30 (1968), 26-39.

Rosenstock, Florence and Kutner, Bernard. "Alienation and Family Crisis," Sociological Quarterly, 9 (1967), 397-405.

Speer, D.C. "Family Systems: Morphostasis and Morphogenesis, or Is Homeostasis Enough," Family Process, 9 (1970), 259-278.

Spiegal, John P. "The Resolution of Role Conflict Within the Family," The Patient and the Mental Hospital, edited by Milton Greenblatt, D.J. Levinson, and R.H. Williams. Glencoe: The Free Press, 1957.

Vogel, Ezra and Bell, Norman W. "The Emotionally Disturbed Child as the Family Scapegoat," The Family, edited by Norman W. Bell and Ezra F. Vogel. Glencoe: The Free Press, 1960.

Waller, Willard and Hill, Reuben. The Family. New York: Holt, Rinehart and Winston, 1951.

Watzlawick, Paul; Beavin, Janet Helmick; and Jackson, Don D. Pragmatics of Human Communication. New York: Norton, 1967.

_____; Weakland, John H.; and Fisch, Richard. Change. New York: Norton, 1974.

SUBJECT INDEX

Abrupt onset of stressor, see Stressor, Onset
Action, 54, 68-70, 72
Alcoholism, 48, 62, 86-87
Appropriate action, 15, 54, 60, 70-71, 72, 73
Appropriate patterns, see Patterns
Awareness, 14, 54, 62-63, 72

Change, 1, 3, 4, 7, 9, 19-23, 27, 54, 69, 70, 74, 81-83, 84,
  86, 93
  orders of change, 8, 28, 84, 86, 89, 97
  pattern change, 17-21, 89
Chronic stressors, see Stressor, Extent
Circular and linear perspectives, 16
Commitment, 72, 78, 90
Communication, 64
Conflict, 23
Consensus, 14, 54, 63, 66-68, 72, 78
Consistency, see Flexibility and Consistency
Consolidation, 15, 91-93, 106
Correction, 14
Crisis definition, 10-12, 21

Death, 38, 62, 63, 67, 71, 101, 103-104, 105
Decision making, 18
Definition of the situation, 14, 31, 34
Developmental framework, 1, 3-4, 16
Developmental crisis, see Normative crisis
Division of labor, 18
Divorce, 96-97, 103
Drift, 20

Effective adaptability, 31
Exits during secondary adjustment, 15, 55, 63, 66, 68

Family
  as acting agents, 21
  as idea, 53
  classified by pattern appropriateness, 26-31
  levels, 22, 24, 28, 48, 78, 82, 88
  non-normative, 99-100
  stability, 81-83
  structure, 111-112
Feedback loops
  negative, 73-74, 83, 84, 85, 89, 115, 117
  positive, 83, 84, 89, 119-120
Financial crisis, 66, 101
Five steps of pattern revision, 14, 25, 34, 54-55, 62-71, 72
Flexibility and consistency, 14, 51, 53-54, 72, 85
Foresight, 40-42, 42-44

Goals, 21, 64
Gradual onset, see Stressor, Onset

129

Homeostasis, 5, 8, 73

Incipience, 11, 12, 31, 37
Information, 69, 118
Instrumentality, see Integration and instrumentality
Intact families, 106
    similarity with modified families, 97-98
Integration and instrumentality, 9, 14, 15, 52-53, 72
Interaction, 18
Interactional stressor, see Stressor, Source

Legal system, 103-105
Levels, see Systems

Modified families
    differences among types, 102-105
    differences among separated families, 105-106
    differences between modified and intact families, 99-105
    similarity with intact families, 97-98
Myths, 88

Nine basic ideas, 9-10
Normative crisis, 31, 40-42

Parenting, 3, 20, 77, 83, 109
Patterns
    appropriate, 11, 22, 23, 23-31, 33, 68, 86, 106
    correction, 23-30, 31, 51, 111
    execution, 23-30, 111
    explained, 18
    inappropriate, 11, 12, 14, 18, 20, 21, 22-23, 33, 54,
        55, 56, 57, 66, 68, 71, 84, 86
Period of incipience, 12, 17-35
Persistence, 1, 8, 17-19, 21, 51, 52-54
Personal level and family level, 22
Priceless unessentials, 52, 61, 95, 110

Quid pro quo, 110

Rebounding, 15, 91, 93-94, 106
Reorganization, 11, 15, 90
Repeat loop, 15, 55, 66, 70
Residues, 94-95
Risk taking, 112
Roles, 18, 93-94
Routes
    through incipience, 26-31
    through secondary adjustment, 14-15, 70-71, 90, 95-96

Scapegoat, 18, 22
Secondary adjustment period, 11, 14, 25, 26, 37, 91
Separated families, differences, 105-106
Separateness - connectedness, 78, 80-81, 82
Speed, 61, 72, 95, 115
Sponsor, 67, 72